Microsoft PowerPoint 2019
in 90 pages

by **Beth Brown**

Belleyre Books

Copyright © 2019 Belleyre Books

All rights reserved. No part of this publication may be reproduced, scanned, or distributed in any printed or electronic form without written consent from the author. The author is the sole owner of the content presented within this text. Photographs copyright Beth Brown, Chris Brown, and Dr. Kristina Jensen.

Published by Belleyre Books
www.belleyrebooks.com

First Edition

ISBN 978-0-9986844-6-8 paperback
ISBN 978-0-9986844-7-5 eBook

Complimentary examination copies are available for educational institutions. Please inquire at www.belleyrebooks.com/contact.

This text is in no way connected with Microsoft Corporation.

Microsoft, Microsoft PowerPoint, Microsoft Word, and Microsoft Excel are either registered trademarks of the Microsoft Corporation in the United States and/or other countries. Screen shots and icons used with permission from Microsoft.

YouTube™ is a registered trademark of Google LLC.

Names of all other products mentioned herein are used for identification purposes only and may be trademarks of their respective owners.

This book was created using Microsoft Word 365.

Revision_1

Also Available

Microsoft Word 2019 in 90 pages

Microsoft PowerPoint 2016 in 90 pages

Microsoft Word 2016 in 90 pages

Microsoft Excel 2016 in 90 pages

Table of Contents

Tables vii
Preface ix
    How to Use this Book ix
    Accessibility Note ix
    About the Author x
Chapter 1 The Basics 1
    Starting PowerPoint 1
    The PowerPoint Interface 1
    The Most Important PowerPoint Feature 4
    Communicating with PowerPoint 6
    The Backstage View 9
    Saving a Presentation 10
    Quitting PowerPoint 10
Chapter 2 Producing a Presentation 11
    First Things First 11
        Planning a Presentation 11
    Creating a New Presentation 12
        Choosing a Presentation Template 12
        Choosing a Slide Size 12
    Adding and Deleting Slides 13
    Adding Slide Content: AutoCorrect, Spell Check, AutoFit,
        and AutoFormat 14
    Inserting Symbols and Equations 17
    Editing Slides 18
    Find and Replace 20
    Formatting Text Content 21
        WordArt 22
    Formatting a Placeholder Object 24
    Format Painter 26
    Creating Speaker Notes 27
    Headers & Footers 28

Changing the Slide Order 29
Review Your Presentation 29
Chapter 3 Presentation Design **31**
Using Themes 31
Slide Master View 33
Transitions 36
The Morph Transition 37
Animations 39
Tables 42
Sections 46
Zoom for Nonlinear Navigation 46
Chapter 4 Graphics, Video, and Audio **47**
Pictures 47
Arranging Objects 51
Text Boxes 52
WordArt Text Boxes 53
Shapes 54
3D Models 53
SmartArt 55
Hyperlinks 57
Action Objects 58
Video 59
Screen Recording Video 62
Audio 64
Chapter 5 Objects, Charts, and Photo Album **67**
Embedding and Linking Objects 67
Linking to Screenshots 70
Charts 70
Photo Album Presentation 74
Chapter 6 Delivering a Presentation **77**
Delivering to a Live Audience 77
Use Timings to Deliver a Presentation 80
Deliver a Presentation as a Recording 82

Chapter 7 Special Purpose PowerPoint Features 85
    Using Multiple Windows 85
    The Draw Tab 86
    Protecting a Presentation 87
    Comments 88
    Collaboration 88
    Creating a Template 89
    Making a Presentation Accessible 90
    Document Inspector 90
Index 91

Tables

Table 1 The PowerPoint Window 3
Table 2 Keyboard Keys and their Functions 6
Table 3 Mouse Actions and Pointer Shapes 8
Table 4 Editing Features 19
Table 5 Reading View Keyboard Shortcuts 30
Table 6 Selecting Slides 32
Table 7 Slide Master Tab 34
Table 8 Table Design tab 43
Table 9 Layout tab 45
Table 10 Object Editing 49
Table 11 Picture Format Tab 49
Table 12 Arranging Multiple Objects 51
Table 13 Shape Format Tab 53
Table 14 Video Tabs 60
Table 15 Playback Tab 66
Table 16 Chart Tabs 73
Table 17 Slide Show Keyboard Shortcuts 79
Table 18 Slide Show Tab 84
Table 19 View Tab Window Group 85
Table 20 Draw Tab 86

Preface

The goal of this book is to provide an approachable learning experience for PowerPoint 2019. Through step-by-step directions, informative tables, and numerous screenshots, you'll be able to master PowerPoint 2019 features to create professional, effective slide show presentations.

Microsoft PowerPoint 2019 in 90 Pages is written for Microsoft PowerPoint 2019 that runs on Windows 10. This text is compatible with PowerPoint 365 but may not cover all 365 features. Contextual tab names may vary between PowerPoint 365 and PowerPoint 2019. The Index lists both contextual tab names, when necessary, with appropriate references. For example: Picture Tools Format tab, *see* Picture Format tab.

How to Use this Book

Chapters divide the features of PowerPoint into related topics with step-by-step instructions for each concept. You can apply these directions to a new presentation or an existing one. References are made throughout the chapters to tables that further detail commands, actions, and features related to a concept.

Refer to the last page of this book for a tear-out PowerPoint 2019 Quick Reference with step-by-step instructions that are keyed to the text. For more information, visit www.belleyrebooks.com.

Accessibility Note

Keyboard shortcuts allow you to keep your hands on the keyboard for faster document development. Some keyboards shortcuts are faster and easier than trying to perform the same action with the mouse. In these cases, the keyboard shortcut is explicitly provided in the instructions.

PowerPoint is an accessible application, and therefore, keyboard shortcuts are provided for essentially every possible command and action. You can determine these shortcuts by viewing the pop-up ScreenTips (p. 7) and by typing "keyboard shortcuts" into the Tell Me search box (p. 4). Further, pressing the Alt key once will display keyboard shortcuts for navigating the tabs and commands on the Ribbon.

About the Author

Beth Brown is the author of more than 40 computer science and computer applications textbooks. An engineering graduate of Florida Atlantic University, Ms. Brown holds a B.S. in Computer Science. She has worked with students and educators worldwide to develop Microsoft Office curriculum materials in addition to her work in programming, research and development, technical writing, and business.

Chapter 1
The Basics

Microsoft PowerPoint 2019 is the ubiquitous slide show application of the Microsoft Office 2019 productivity suite. PowerPoint is essential to anyone who intends to present information to an audience, whether it be with a slide show, a PowerPoint video, or a packaged presentation.

Starting PowerPoint

How you start PowerPoint will depend on your device, but you will usually need to click the PowerPoint 2019 icon in the Taskbar at the bottom of a PC screen or double-click the icon on the Desktop. If you don't see the PowerPoint icon, click the Start menu in the lower-left corner of your screen and scroll through the list to locate the PowerPoint 2019 icon (you may need to expand the Microsoft Office 2019 folder) or type *PowerPoint* into the Search box on the Taskbar.

The PowerPoint Interface

The PowerPoint *application interface* refers to the area where you interact with PowerPoint. When you start PowerPoint, the interface, also called the PowerPoint window, displays the Start screen where you can choose to create a new presentation or open an existing presentation.

In the Start screen (Figure 1, p. 2), click Blank Presentation to create a new slide show. A new presentation contains one blank slide. Or, click a link under Recent to open a file you've already created. You Start screen may be organized differently but will have the same features.

The PowerPoint window with a new presentation looks similar to Figure 2, p. 2. Refer to Table 1, p. 3 for information about the features.

Figure 1 The Start screen.

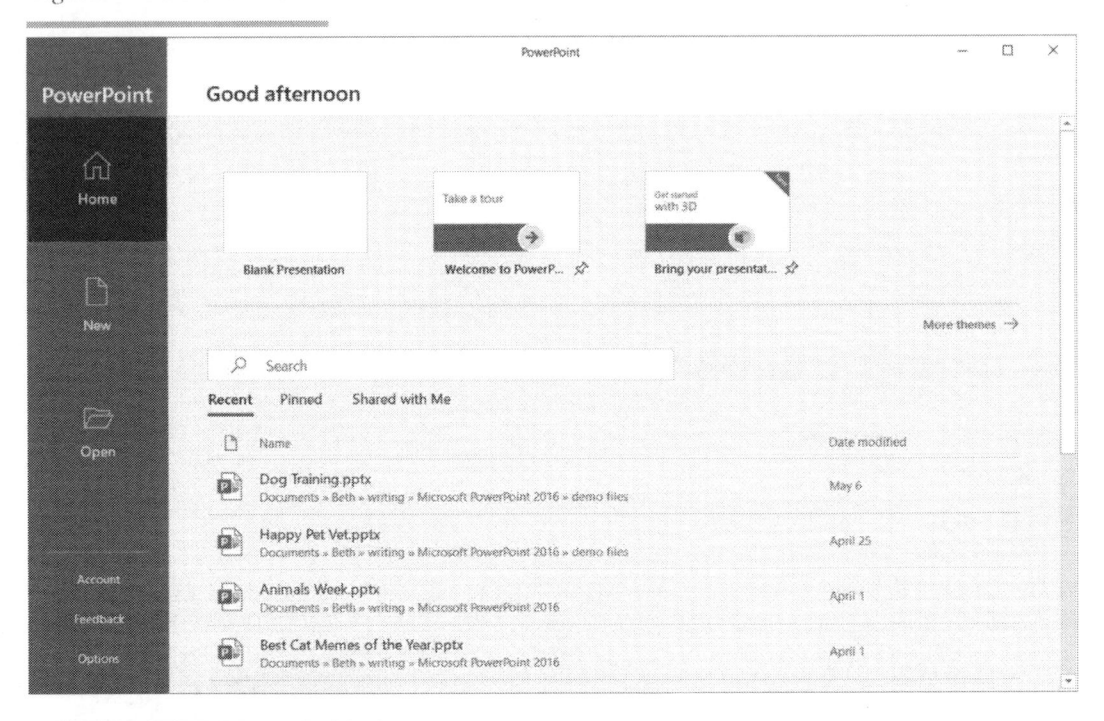

Figure 2 A new presentation.

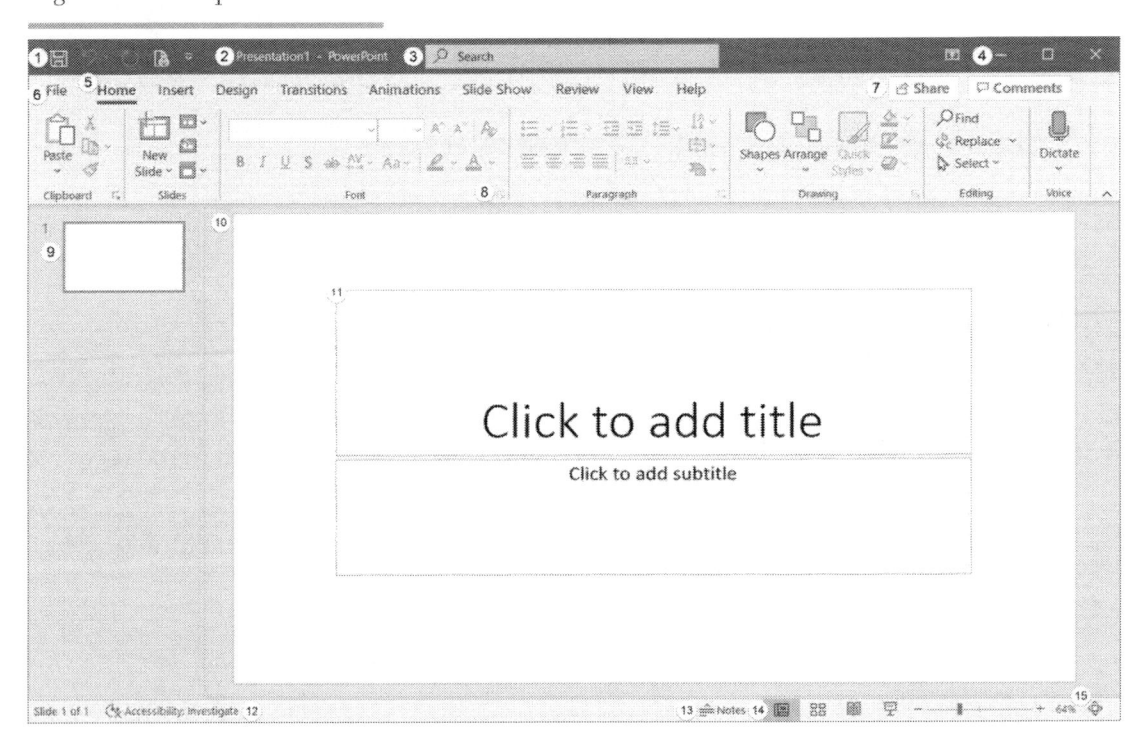

Table 1 The PowerPoint Window

①	**Quick Access toolbar**	Save, Undo, Redo, Print Preview and Print, Customize Quick Access Toolbar. Refer also to p. 19.
②	**File name**	This is the name of your presentation. Presentation1 is the default name until you save your file with a more descriptive name.
③	**Tell Me box**	A help and search feature. The Tell Me box may alternatively appear after the last Ribbon tab. Refer to p. 4.
④	**Window controls**	Minimize and Maximize window size. Close the window with the X button.
⑤	**Ribbon**	The Ribbon is divided into tabs that group commands (File, Home, Insert, Design, Transitions, Animations, Slide Show, Review, View and Help tabs and possibly a Draw tab). Click the Ribbon Display Options button, near the window controls, to hide the Ribbon or reduce the Ribbon to just tabs.
⑥	**File tab**	Click to display the Backstage view where you can open, close, save as, print, and distribute your presentation. Refer also to p. 9.
⑦	**Share and Comments**	Collaborate with others on a presentation. See and respond to comments. Refer to Chapter 7.
⑧	**Dialog box launcher**	Click to display a dialog box with options for a Ribbon group or open a task pane.
⑨	**Thumbnail**	Miniature of a slide. The *active* thumbnail displays a heavy outline and corresponds to the current slide in the Slide pane. Drag a thumbnail up or down to change the order of the slides in a presentation. Press the Delete key to remove the active slide.
⑩	**Slide pane**	Displays the current slide.

⑪ **Content placeholder**	Click in a content placeholder to type text, insert a table, add images, charts, or video or sound clips. Content placeholders can be sized, positioned, and deleted.
⑫ **Accessibility**	Click Accessibility to open a pane with tips for making a presentation accessible to people with disabilities.
⑬ **Notes**	Click Notes to open a Notes pane in the Slides pane. Here, speaker notes, which aren't visible to the audience, are typed for reference when delivering a presentation. Refer also to p. 27.
⑭ **View options**	Click Normal, Slide Sorter, Reading View, or Slide Show in the status bar to change the way you view your slides.
⑮ **Zoom controls**	Drag the slider or click – or + to change slide magnification. You can also click the Zoom level to display a dialog box.

TIP The Presentation Views and Zoom options are also available on the View tab.

TIP Drag the divider between the thumbnails and the Slide pane to increase or decrease the thumbnail size.

The Most Important PowerPoint Feature

The Tell Me box is probably the most important PowerPoint feature to know about. It is a powerful search and help tool that appears above the Ribbon tab. It's symbolized by a magnifying glass with the text Search (Figure 3). In some cases, the text may be Tell me what you want to do.

Figure 3 The Tell Me box.

Chapter 1 The Basics 5

When you click Search (or Tell me what you want to do) and then type a word or phrase, PowerPoint suggests related commands (Figure 4).

Figure 4 Search text in the Tell Me box displays a menu of options.

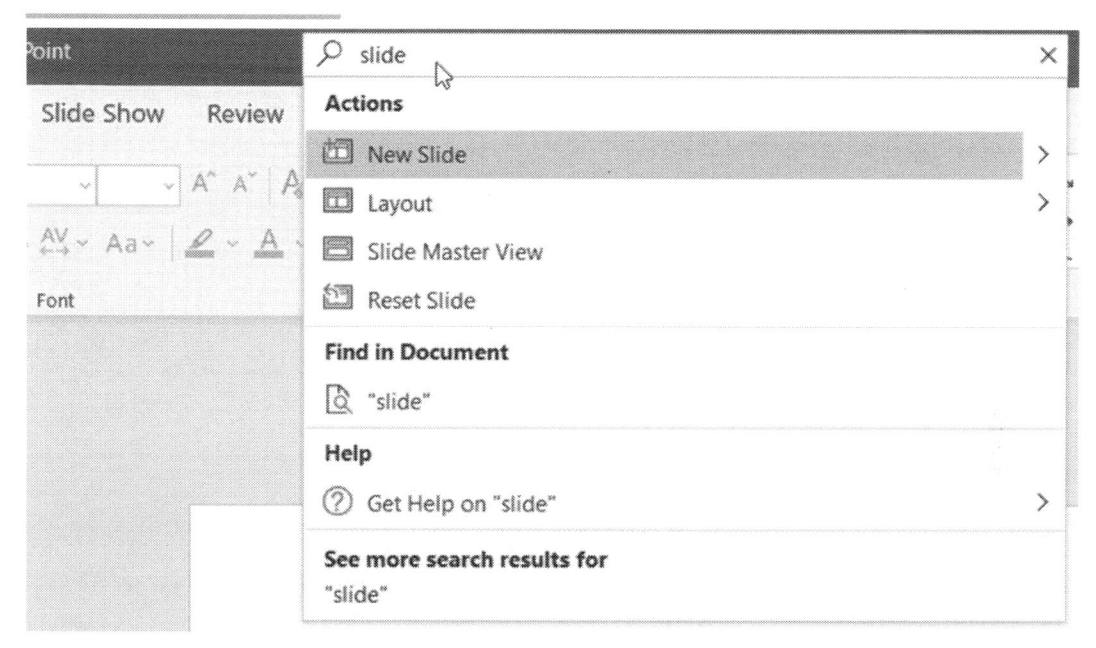

The Tell Me results menu is context sensitive. Different commands and actions will be displayed depending on what's going on in your presentation.

At the bottom of the Tell Me results menu, there are options to display Help and perform a search for more results. These commands open a *pane*, which is a set of options that remains open with your presentation. To close the pane, you click Close X in its upper-right corner.

The Tell Me box is the most important PowerPoint feature because you no longer need to remember which Ribbon tab holds a command or which button is which — you can just get to work and ask PowerPoint for whatever it is you need.

TIP Use the Index in the back of this book to quickly locate information for a PowerPoint feature.

TIP Refer to the tear-out Quick Reference at the back of this book for step-by-step instructions for commonly performed actions.

Communicating with PowerPoint

Input devices are needed so that you can communicate with PowerPoint. The devices you are most likely to use are the keyboard and mouse.

To add text to a slide, click in a content placeholder to make it *active* and then type. As you press keys on the keyboard, characters appear in the placeholder at the location of the blinking line called the insertion point (Figure 5).

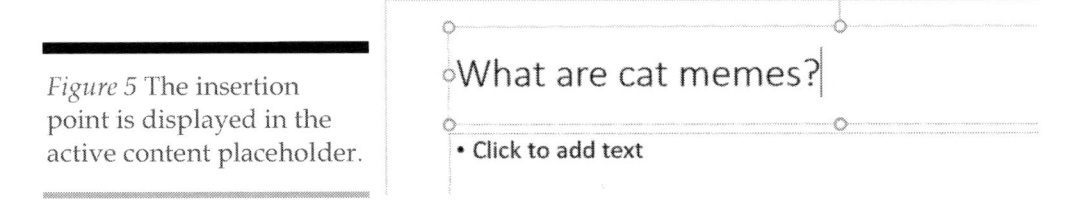

Figure 5 The insertion point is displayed in the active content placeholder.

Special keys on the keyboard are used to control the insertion point position, while the Escape key allows you to cancel an action, such as the display of a dialog box. The Ctrl key is used in combination with other keys to perform an action. Refer to Table 2.

Table 2 Keyboard Keys and their Functions

Key	Function
Esc	Press the Escape (Esc) key to cancel the current action.
Ctrl	The Control (Ctrl) key is used in combination with other keys. You must press and hold the Ctrl key before pressing a second key. For example, Ctrl+S means to press and hold Ctrl while pressing the S key once.
Arrow keys	Press an arrow key to position the insertion point. Press Ctrl+arrow key to move the insertion point from word to word or line to line.
Tab	Press Tab to move the insertion point to the next tab stop or to change the bullet level of a list.
Enter	Press Enter to move the insertion point to the next line or to create a new bullet item.

Chapter 1 The Basics 7

Home	Press Home to move the insertion point to the beginning of a line of text.
End	Press End to move the insertion point to the end of a line of text.
Page Up Page Down	The Page Up (PgUp) and Page Down (PgDn) keys are used to scroll slides.
Delete	Press the Delete key to remove characters to the right of the insertion point. Delete is also uses to remove selected objects.
←Backspace	The Backspace key removes characters to the left of the insertion point.

The mouse is a pointing device that displays a graphic image called a *pointer*. You can use the mouse to select commands on the Ribbon, respond to prompts, select objects such as content placeholders, and position the insertion point for editing text. When you rest (point) the mouse pointer on a command or feature of the interface a helpful *ScreenTip* pops up, as shown in Figure 6.

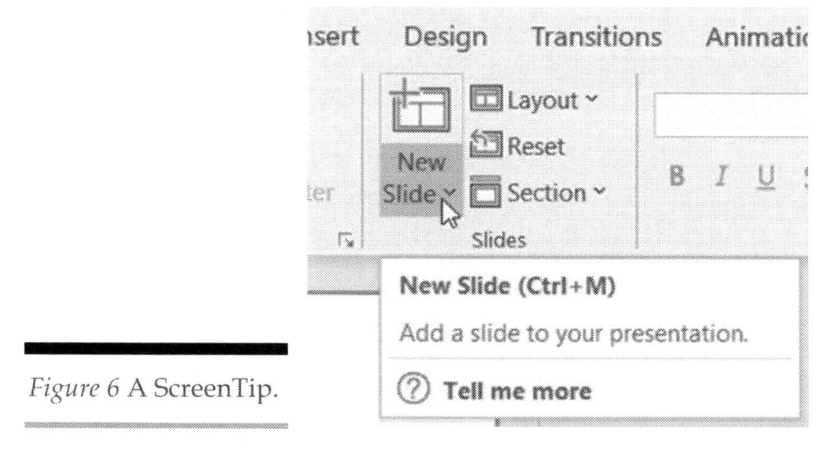

Figure 6 A ScreenTip.

The pointer shape changes depending on where the pointer is placed. One exception is when PowerPoint is working on an action, which is indicated by an hourglass pointer. You can further communicate with PowerPoint through different actions using the mouse buttons. These actions and mouse pointer shapes are described in Table 3, p. 8.

Table 3 Mouse Actions and Pointer Shapes

Point	Move the mouse until the pointer is placed on an object or in a specific area.
Click	Press and release the left mouse button once.
Double-click	Press and release the left mouse button twice in rapid succession.
Right-click	Press and release the right mouse button once.
Drag	Press and hold the left mouse button while moving the mouse. This action positions an object or highlights text.
Scroll wheel	If available, rotate the scroll wheel up or down to bring different slides into view.
▷	The arrow pointer is displayed when the mouse pointer is positioned over a command or other clickable object.
✥	The four-headed arrow pointer appears when you point to the dotted border of a content placeholder and other objects. Drag the border with this pointer to reposition the object.
⤡	The two-headed arrow pointer appears when you point to a handle of a selected object. Drag the handle with this pointer to size the object.
I	The I-beam pointer is displayed when the mouse pointer is in an area where text can be typed. Click the I-beam to place the insertion point.
👆	The hand shape is typical when the mouse pointer is positioned over a hyperlink. Click to follow a link.

The Backstage View

The File tab on the PowerPoint Ribbon displays the *Backstage view*. From here, you work with files, print, and set PowerPoint options, among other things. You can click ⬅ at any time or press the Escape key when you want to return to your presentation. Click a command on the left side of Backstage view to display related options:

Info displays the properties and other information about your presentation. Chapter 7 discusses inspecting the presentation.

New displays options for creating a new presentation, including templates which are discussed further in Chapters 2 and 7.

Open displays links to recently opened files. Click Browse to display the Open dialog box where you can navigate to other files.

Save is discussed on p. 10. Save As is used to save a copy of a presentation with a new name. If you want to save the copy in a new location, click Browse and then navigate to the desired folder in the Save As dialog box. You also have the option of changing the file format to PDF or another file type when you click the Save as type list below the File name box in the dialog box.

Print displays a print preview with options for selecting your printer and changing print settings, which include printing all slides, the current slide, or several slides to a page.

Share displays options for emailing your presentation or making it available to others for editing or viewing. Click Email to send your presentation as a PowerPoint attachment or as a PDF attachment. Refer also to Chapter 7 for more on sharing.

Export has options for creating a PDF, creating a video (including Ultra HD 4K), packaging a presentation, and creating handouts. There are also options for converting a presentation file to a different file type. When a file is exported, the original remains, and a new file is created.

Close removes your presentation from the PowerPoint window without closing PowerPoint.

Account displays information about your version of PowerPoint.

Options displays the PowerPoint Options dialog box for customizing how PowerPoint interacts with you. With this dialog box you can access options related to proofing, auto save, AutoCorrect, the Ribbon, and the Quick Access toolbar.

Saving a Presentation

You will want to save your presentation frequently — every minute or two if you're doing a lot of typing and editing. Saving often is so important that PowerPoint provides several ways to execute the action:

- The Save command on the File tab. However, this is a rather weighty way to have to get to a command you want to execute often.
- The Save button 🖫 on the Quick Access toolbar (Figure 2, p. 2). The first time this button is clicked, you will be prompted for the location from a dialog box or from the Backstage view. Clicking 🖫 with a named presentation simply updates the file with your changes without showing a dialog box.
- And if you want to keep your hands on the keyboard, press Ctrl+S to save your presentation (press and hold the Ctrl key and then press the S key once).

Quitting PowerPoint

If you are ready to quit PowerPoint and close the application interface, click Close X in the upper-right corner of the PowerPoint window. If you've made unsaved changes to an open presentation, you will be prompted to either save or discard the changes before quitting.

Chapter 2
Producing a Presentation

A slide show presentation is a *production*. It's a creative work that involves starting PowerPoint, choosing a template, and then adding slides that are formatted and organized to present your ideas most effectively.

First Things First

Planning a Presentation

The effectiveness of a presentation directly correlates to the quality of its content. And just to be clear, slide transitions, sound effects, and wild colors do not count as content. Always plan your presentation before attempting to create one in PowerPoint. Without a plan, you may find yourself trying to shore up weak content with PowerPoint bells and whistles that don't stand a chance of impacting your audience.

A presentation should tell a story. It will have a beginning, a middle, and an end. Keep this in mind when using the following steps to plan a presentation:

1. **Determine the purpose of the presentation.** Do you want to persuade an audience or strictly inform them?
2. **Gather your content.** What information do you want to convey (keeping your purpose in mind)? Do you have charts, tables, videos, or sound clips that support your content? Do you need to include a company logo or other images?
3. **Decide how to organize the content into slides.** This involves deciding on a slide design, separating content into slides and speaker notes, and making sure there is a logical progression from start to finish.

TIP The number of slides in a presentation will vary, but a good start is to consider slides for the presentation title, an introduction, each of the main points, a summary, and a call to action. A *call to action* inspires your audience to act on the information you've presented. Phrases that begin with "Reserve now...", "Ask me...", or "Don't wait..." are commonly used.

Creating a New Presentation

When creating a new presentation, you will need to choose the presentation template and then the slide size.

Choosing a Presentation Template

Whether you're at the PowerPoint Start screen or the File ⇨ New screen, you'll need to decide which template you want to use for your new presentation. A *template* is a file that already has a theme and several slide layouts. PowerPoint Blank Presentation is the most basic template, providing a plain theme with several slide layouts. Customizing a template and theme is explained in Chapter 3. Creating your own template is discussed in Chapter 7.

Choosing a Slide Size

The default PowerPoint slide size is Widescreen 16:9 aspect ratio. This size is applicable to most situations. The Standard 4:3 aspect ratio is a good choice for presentations that are better suited to a squarer slide size. PowerPoint also offers many custom sizes that match, for example, a letter size paper or an overhead projector. You can change the slide size at any time, but if you've already created slides, you will need to check that all the content is still visible.

To create a new presentation:

1. Start PowerPoint and click Blank Presentation on the right side of the Start screen. A new presentation is displayed with an empty Title Slide. As you continue through this chapter, you will learn the remaining steps to completing the presentation.

2. *Optional*. Click the Design tab and in the Themes group, click More to display built-in themes. Click a theme to change the overall design of the presentation. (Themes are discussed in Chapter 3.)

3. *Optional*. Click Design ⇨ Slide Size in the Customize group and choose Standard for a squarer slide size. Or click Design ⇨ Slide Size ⇨ Custom Slide Size for a dialog box where you can choose an option in the Slides sized for list (click the list arrow) or enter your own Width, Height, and Orientation.

Chapter 2 Producing a Presentation

Adding and Deleting Slides

A new presentation has one slide, a Title Slide with content placeholders for a title and a subtitle. There are numerous built-in slide layouts to choose from for additional slides (Figure 7). Available layouts will depend on the selected theme:

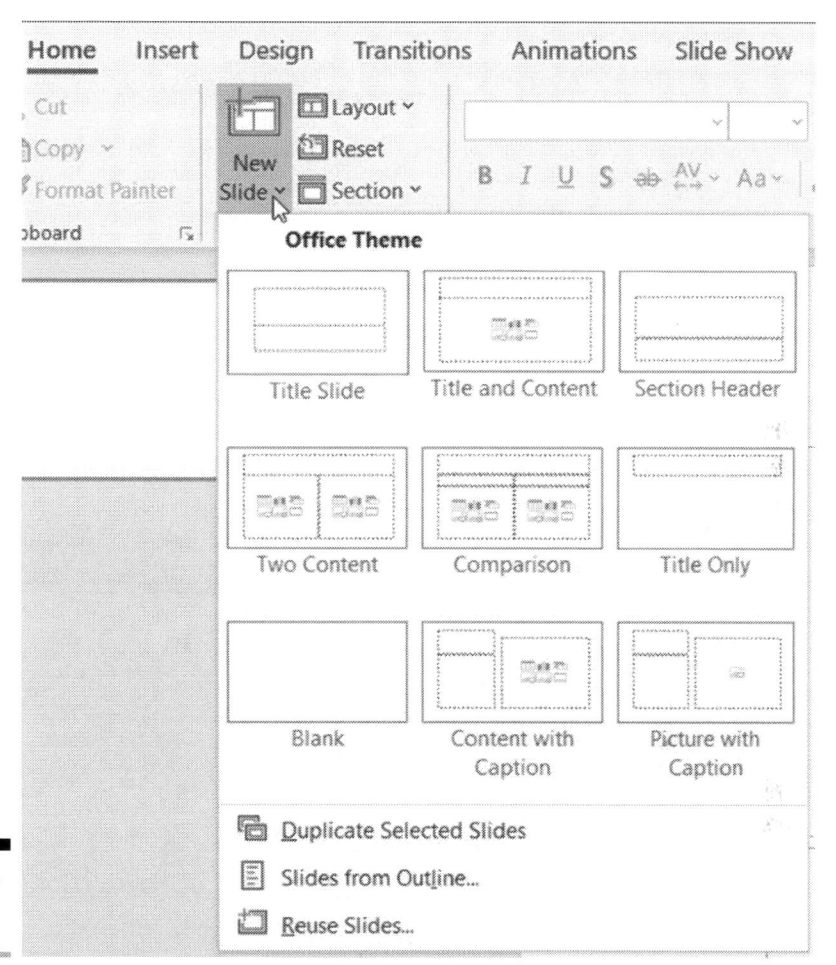

Figure 7 The New Slide gallery.

To add a slide to a presentation:

1. Click the slide thumbnail that is to come before the new slide. The selected thumbnail displays a heavy border (as shown on p. 2).
2. Click the Home ⇨ New Slide arrow (refer to Figure 7 above). A gallery of slide layouts is displayed.

3. Click a slide layout to add it to the presentation.

   Or

   Click Duplicate Selected Slides to add a duplicate of the selected thumbnail.

4. *Optional.* To change the layout of an inserted slide, be sure its thumbnail is selected and then click Home ⇨ Layout and select a different slide layout.

To delete a slide from a presentation:

1. Click a thumbnail. The selected thumbnail displays a heavy border.
2. Press the Delete key.

TIP Click Home ⇨ New Slide (not the arrow) to add a slide with the same layout as the selected thumbnail.

TIP Click Home ⇨ New Slide ⇨ Reuse Slides to select slides from an existing presentation.

TIP To add slides based on a Word document outline (View ⇨ Outline in Word), click Home ⇨ New Slide ⇨ Slides from Outline and then click Home ⇨ Reset for each of the new slides.

TIP Right-click a thumbnail for New Slide, Duplicate Slide, Delete Slide, and Layout commands.

Adding Slide Content: AutoCorrect, Spell Check, AutoFit, and AutoFormat

Slides often include titles, bullet items, and other forms of text. But keep in mind that slides are meant to support your narration, not transcribe it. Few words, a limited number of slides (a presentation that runs about 20 minutes is ideal), and images that trigger emotion usually garner the best response. (Chapter 4 explains how to add graphic, video, and audio content. Chapter 5 explains how to add pre-existing content from other files.)

The slide in Figure 8 has title text in a text placeholder at the top and a bulleted list in the content placeholder below. The *active* content placeholder contains the insertion point and displays *handles*.

Chapter 2 Producing a Presentation 15

Figure 8 A slide with text content.

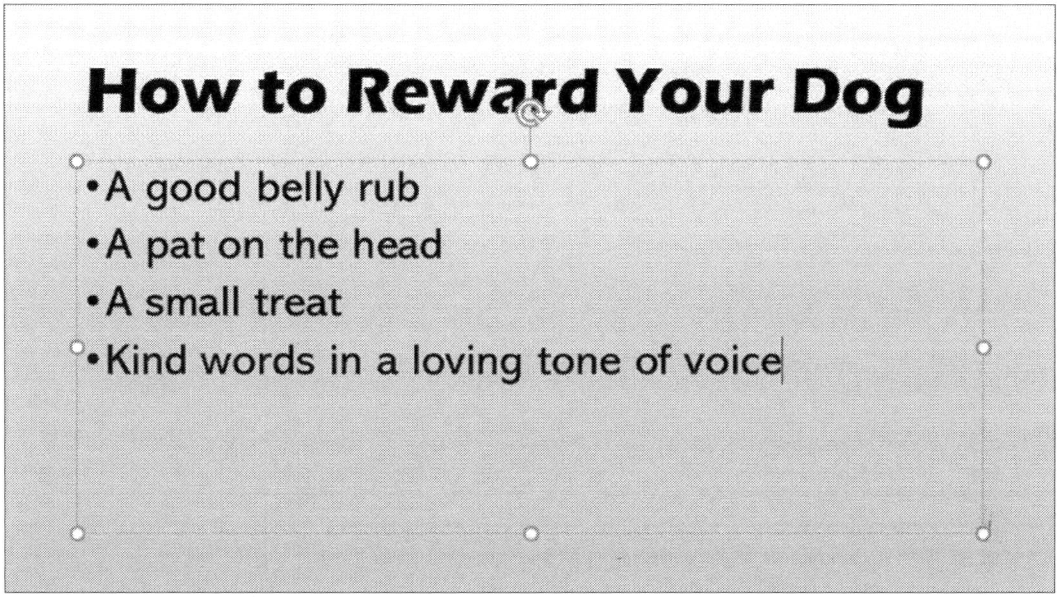

How to Reward Your Dog

- A good belly rub
- A pat on the head
- A small treat
- Kind words in a loving tone of voice

To add text to a slide:

1. Click the thumbnail of the slide to edit. The slide is displayed in the Slide pane.

2. Click in a placeholder and type your text. PowerPoint assists you with the AutoCorrect, AutoFit, and AutoFormat features along with the spelling checker, which are described on pages 16 and 17.

3. If you're adding text to a content placeholder formatted with bullets:

    - Type text for the first bullet item and then press Enter at the end of the line of text to create the next bullet item.

    - To change a bullet style or remove bullets entirely, select bullet text and then click the ≔ or ≔ arrow on the Home tab for options.

    - To change the bullet level, press Tab at the start of the item or click ≔ or ≔ on the Home tab.

As you type, the PowerPoint *AutoCorrect* feature compares the characters you type to a list and then automatically makes changes when there is a match. For example, when you type adn, it is converted to "and"; ahve is converted to "have". AutoCorrect also converts specified character sequences to special characters. For example, when you type (c), it is converted to ©. Similarly, (r) is changed to ® and (tm) is changed to ™. 1/2 is changed to ½ and 1/4 converts to ¼. To reverse an AutoCorrect action, press Ctrl+Z immediately after it happens.

To view the AutoCorrect list and edit entries:

1. Click File ⇨ Options ⇨ Proofing ⇨ AutoCorrect Options. The dialog box displays a scrollable AutoCorrect list. (Click the AutoCorrect tab in the dialog box, if necessary.)

2. To add a new entry, type the appropriate text in the Replace and With boxes and then click Add.

3. To remove an existing entry, click the entry in the list and then click Delete.

PowerPoint displays a red squiggly line under characters not matching a word in the dictionary file or in the AutoCorrect list.

To correct a red flagged word or phrase (spelling error):

1. Right-click the text. A menu is displayed similar to Figure 9.

Figure 9 The right-click spelling menu.

2. Click a correctly spelled word to replace the unknown word.

   Or

   Click Ignore All to remove the squiggly line from this and every occurrence of the spelling in the presentation.

   Or

   Click Add to Dictionary to remove the squiggly line and add the word to the dictionary file so that it will be recognized in all future presentations.

3. *Optional.* To change or view spelling options, click File ⇨ Options ⇨ Proofing.

The PowerPoint *AutoFit* feature sizes text as you type so that it fits within the original placeholder. Before you drag a size handle to make the placeholder larger, you may first want to consider eliminating some text from the slide. PowerPoint slides should be used to guide your presentation, not list every word you plan to say. To control Autofit options, click the ⇕ button that appears to the left of a placeholder with reduced text and select a command.

AutoFit is one of several PowerPoint *AutoFormat* features. As you type, changes such as straight quotes to curly quotes are also made. To see all the AutoFormat options, click File ⇨ Options ⇨ Proofing ⇨ AutoCorrect Options and then click the AutoFormat As You Type tab.

Inserting Symbols and Equations

When your slide needs to include a character or symbol that isn't on the keyboard, such as á or ¢, you use Insert ⇨ Symbol in the Symbols group (Figure 10) to add the symbol at the insertion point. The command displays a dialog box with symbols and special characters.

Figure 10 The Symbols group on the Insert tab.

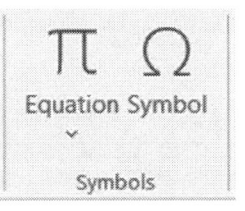

To insert an equation:

1. Click in a content placeholder to place the insertion point at the location for the equation.
2. Click the Insert ⇨ Equation arrow. A gallery is displayed.
3. Click an existing equation. The equation is inserted, and the Equation tab is displayed. To edit the equation, type or use the Equation tab tools.

   Or

   Click Insert New Equation. An equation placeholder is inserted, and the Equation tab is displayed. Type the equation or use the Equation tab tools to insert the equation.

Or

Click Ink Equation. A dialog box is displayed for you to draw an equation and then click Insert to add it to the slide.

TIP To insert a floating equation object, click Insert ⇨ Equation when there are no selected placeholders. Objects are discussed further in Chapter 4.

TIP Equations can also be created using the Draw tab. Refer to Chapter 7.

Editing Slides

Edits to your presentation are almost always required to attain a polished, effective slide show. Editing involves changing, deleting, and moving text and objects. Refer also to Figure 12 and Table 4 on p. 19.

To edit slides:

1. Most edits to text require that you first select, or highlight, the block of text.

    Selecting text is the process of dragging the mouse over text to highlight it, as in Figure 11. (Refer to Table 4, p. 19 for other methods to select text.) If you need to clear the selection, click anywhere outside the highlighted text.

    Figure 11 Selected text is highlighted.   •Overall fun-loving

    Or

    Edits to a text placeholder require that you first select the object.

    To *select a placeholder*, click in the placeholder to display its dotted border and then click the border with the four-headed arrow pointer. The border turns to a solid line and the insertion point is no longer displayed.

2. If you want to **delete** a selection, press the Delete key.

3. If you want to **move** a selection to another slide, click Home ⇨ Cut. The selection is removed from the slide. Next, click the thumbnail of the slide to receive the selection, place the insertion point where you want the moved text, if necessary, and then click Home ⇨ Paste.

Chapter 2 Producing a Presentation 19

4. If you want to **duplicate** a selection, click Home ⇨ Copy. The original selection is left in place. Next, click the thumbnail of the slide to receive the selection, place the insertion point where you want the copied text, if necessary, and then click Home ⇨ Paste.

5. Save (Ctrl+S) your slide show often during the editing process!

Editing commands are in the upper-left of the PowerPoint window, in the Quick Access toolbar and on the Home tab, as shown in Figure 12. The Cut and Copy commands place selected text onto the *Clipboard*, a storage area in memory, which can be accessed while the presentation is open in PowerPoint.

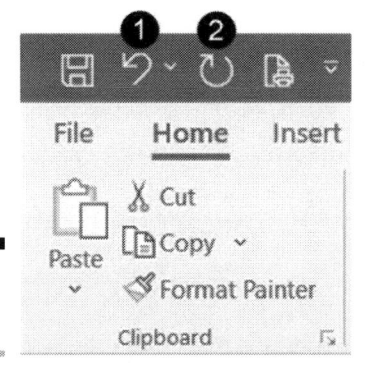

Figure 12
Editing tools.

Table 4 Editing Features

① **Undo**	Click to reverse the most recent action. Click the Undo arrow to choose from a list of actions to reverse.
② **Redo**	Click to reverse the last Undo.
Home ⇨ Cut	Click Cut (Ctrl+X) to remove a selection and place it on the Clipboard.
Home ⇨ Copy	Click Copy (Ctrl+C) to place a duplicate of a selection onto the Clipboard, leaving the original selection unchanged.
Home ⇨ Paste	Click Paste (Ctrl+V) to place the last cut or copied selection on the slide. The Paste Options (Ctrl) button appears after pasting to allow you to choose how you want the item placed on the slide.

Home ⇨ Clipboard dialog box launcher	Click the dialog box launcher to open the Clipboard task pane. Click an item on the Clipboard to place it at the insertion point.
Block selection	Drag the mouse pointer from one character to another to select a block of text. Alternatively, press and hold Shift and then click to select every character between the insertion point and where you click.
Word selection	Double-click the mouse pointer on a word to select the word and the space after.
Paragraph selection	Triple-click in text to select an entire bullet point of text.
Home ⇨ Select	Click Select All to select all the text in the active placeholder. Otherwise, Select All selects all the objects on a slide. Click Selection Pane to display a list of the objects for the current slide.
Backspace	Press to remove a character to the left of the insertion point or to remove a selected block of text.
Delete	Press to remove a character to the right of the insertion point or to remove a selected block of text.

Find and Replace

The Find command makes easy work of locating a slide with a specified word or phrase. Even more powerful is the Replace command for locating and changing text. You can even switch out one font for another with this command.

To find and replace text:

1. Click Home ⇨ Find. A dialog box is displayed.
2. In the Find what box, type the text you want to locate.
3. Click Find Next. The first slide with the find what text is displayed in the Slide pane with the find text selected.

Chapter 2 Producing a Presentation 21

4. If you want to replace text with other text, click Replace. The dialog box expands to display a Replace with box.
5. Type replace text and then click Replace. The find text is replaced and the next occurrence is selected.
6. Continue to click Replace until all the specified find text is substituted.
7. To reverse changes, click Ctrl+Z for each replacement.

To find and replace fonts:

1. Click the Home ⇨ Replace arrow and then click Replace Fonts. A dialog box is displayed.
2. Click the Replace box arrow and select one of the fonts in your presentation.
3. Click the With arrow and select a font.
4. Click Replace to change the text formats matching the replace font to the with font, and then click Close.
5. To reverse the font change, immediately press Ctrl+Z or click Undo .

TIP Click Home ⇨ Replace to immediately display the Replace dialog box.

Formatting Text Content

The goal in formatting text is to make it easier to comprehend. With a presentation, you will also want to keep slides from being unnecessarily complicated. PowerPoint provides numerous character and paragraph formats; Your job is to choose which works with your audience. Some considerations:

- Rarely will you ever need to use more than two or three fonts.
- Keeping the font size at 30 points or greater will allow easy reading for most viewers.
- Fonts are classified as serif (with small lines at the ends of a letter) and **sans serif** (without small lines). Slides are usually best read in a sans serif font.

To format text on a slide:

1. Select the text to format (p. 18).

2. Click commands on the Home tab in the Font and Paragraph group. (First point to a button for more information about a command. Click a command arrow ⌄ for more options.) Refer to Figure 13. (Text Highlighter may appear as ᵃᵇ⌄ or ✎⌄)

Or

Click commands on the mini toolbar (available when you use the mouse to select text). Refer to Figure 14.

Or

Click the dialog box launcher ⌞ in the Font or Paragraph groups on the Home tab to set options from a dialog box.

Figure 13 Text formatting commands on the Home tab.

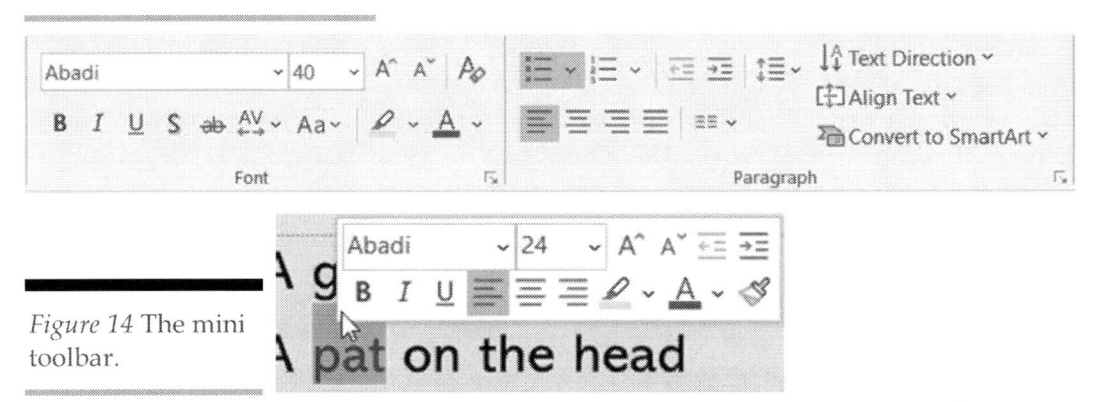

Figure 14 The mini toolbar.

WordArt

WordArt is a PowerPoint feature that formats text with fill patterns, outlines, and effects. Use WordArt sparingly to effectively emphasize text without distracting from the overall message. Always consider the readability of WordArt formats on your audience.

To apply WordArt formats to text on a slide:

1. Select the text to format.
2. Click Shape Format ⇨ ⌄ in the WordArt Styles group (Figure 15).

Figure 15 The More button.

Chapter 2 Producing a Presentation 23

3. Point to a style in the gallery for a preview. Click a style to apply the format.
4. *Optional.* Click Text Fill, Text Outline, and Text Effects formatting commands in the WordArt Styles group for other formats. Multiple formats can be applied to the same text.

   Or

   Click 🔽 in the WordArt Styles group to open the Format Shape task pane with Text Options (Figure 16).

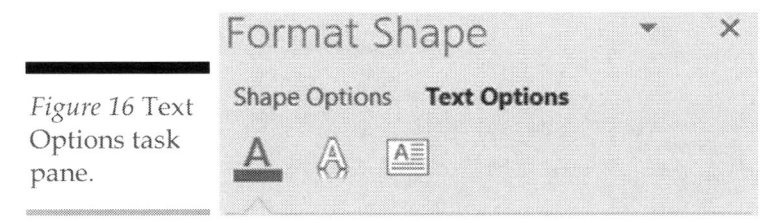

Figure 16 Text Options task pane.

   a) Click the Text Fill & Outline A , Text Effects A , or Textbox A icon at the top of the task pane to display related options.
   b) Below a selected icon, click a white triangle to expand an option group. In Figure 17, Text Outline has been expanded.

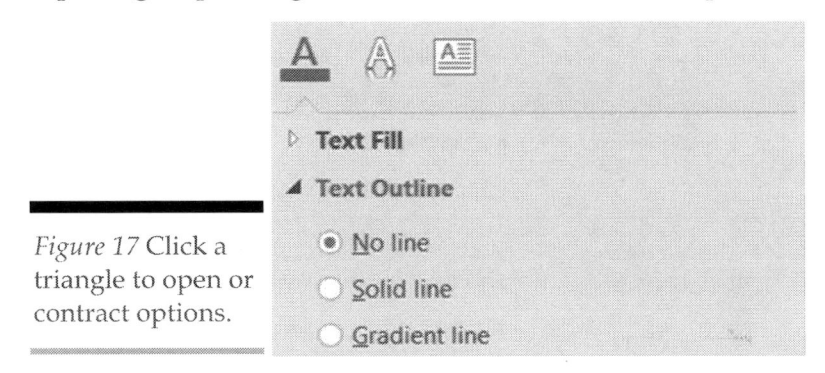

Figure 17 Click a triangle to open or contract options.

5. If you want to remove WordArt styles from selected text, click ⇨ Clear WordArt in the WordArt Styles group.

TIP When you want to apply the same format to text on every slide, use the Slide Master view (Chapter 3).

TIP Carefully choose styles. Underline may lead a reader to think you are providing a link, and too many colors can be confusing.

TIP Chapter 4 explains how to insert floating WordArt text boxes.

Formatting a Placeholder Object

A placeholder has object properties for color, size, text box margins, and more. Shape fill refers to the color of the placeholder background, as demonstrated in Figure 18.

Figure 18 The left placeholder has a black shape fill.

How to Reward Your Dog

- A good belly rub
- A pat on the head
- A small treat
- Kind words in a loving tone of voice

To format a placeholder object:

1. Click in a placeholder. Handles are displayed.
2. Click commands on the Home tab in the Drawing group (Figure 19) to change the background (Shape Fill), border (Shape Outline), and visual effects (Shape Effects). Click Quick Styles for sets of formats. (Point to a button for more information. Click a command arrow ˅ for more options.)

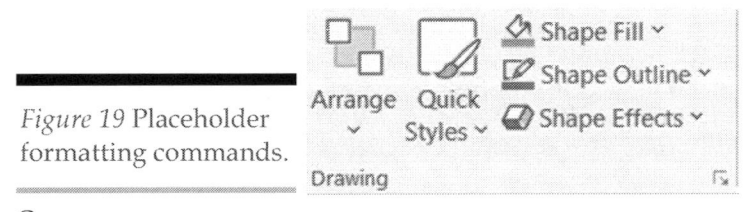

Figure 19 Placeholder formatting commands.

Or

Chapter 2 Producing a Presentation

Click the Shape Format tab and use commands in the Shape Styles, Arrange, and Size groups.

Or

Click the Shape Format tab and then click ⬚ in the Shape Styles, Arrange, or Size groups to open the Format Shape task pane with Shape Options.

a) Click the Fill & Line, Effects, or Size & Properties icon at the top of the task pane to display related options. In Figure 20 the Size & Properties icon is selected.

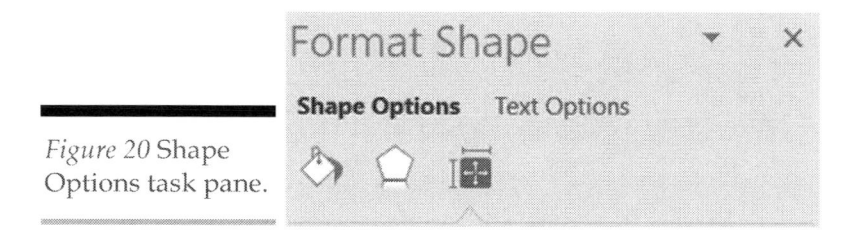

Figure 20 Shape Options task pane.

b) Below a selected icon, click a white triangle to expand an option group. Text Box has been expanded in Figure 21.

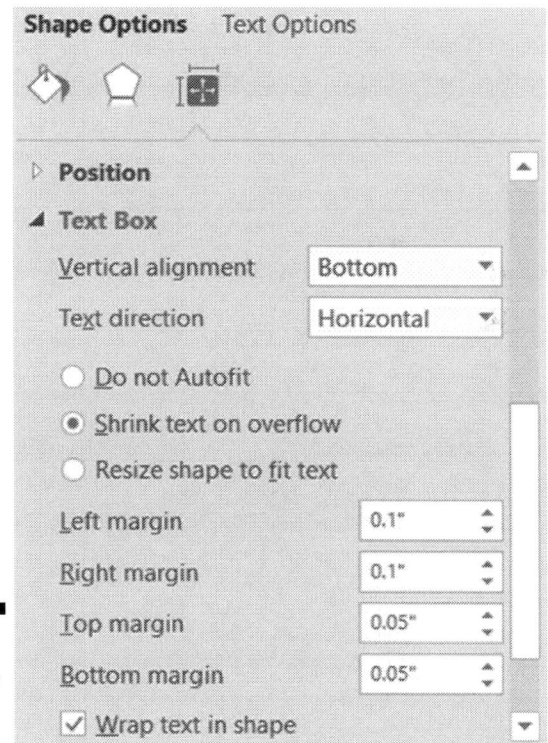

Figure 21 Click a triangle to open or contract options.

TIP Click Home ⇨ Reset to revert the position, size, and formatting of a slide's placeholders to the default settings.

TIP For a more consistent look, format placeholder objects from Slide Master view (Chapter 3).

Format Painter

The Format Painter command on the Home tab in the Clipboard group is a time-saving way to create consistent formats on your slides. Its ScreenTip serves as a reminder of how to use the command (Figure 22).

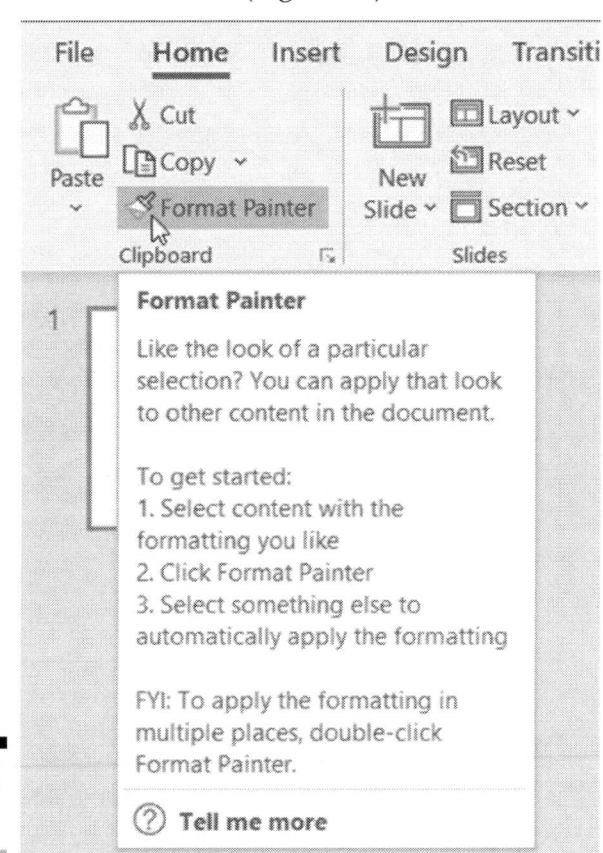

Figure 22 The Format Painter command.

To copy formats:

    1. Select the text with the formats you want to copy.

       Or

Chapter 2 Producing a Presentation 27

Select the placeholder with the formats you want to copy by clicking in the placeholder to display its dotted border and then clicking the border with the four-headed arrow pointer. The border turns to a solid line and the insertion point is no longer displayed.

2. Click Home ⇨ Format Painter.
3. Click the thumbnail of the slide to receive the format.
4. When you move the mouse pointer onto the Slide pane, the Format Painter pointer is displayed. Click text or a placeholder to apply the formatting.

TIP If you want to apply the same formats in several locations, double-click Format Painter when copying the formats and then click once in each destination location. When you no longer want to paste formats, press the Esc key.

Creating Speaker Notes

Speaker notes are used to remind you of what you want to say about each slide. They are displayed in Presenter View when your computer is connected to a projector. The notes can be viewed by you while your audience sees only the slide. Delivering a presentation is explained in Chapter 6.

To add speaker notes to the current slide:

1. In the status bar, click ≜ Notes. The Notes pane is displayed for the current slide (Figure 23).

Figure 23 Click Notes for the Notes pane.

2. Click in the Notes pane and type your speaker notes. Remember they will only be visible to you during a presentation.

TIP Drag the border above the Notes pane to make it larger. You can also click View ⇨ Notes Page for a larger text box to type your notes.

TIP Speaker notes are there to remind you of how you want to talk through your bullet points or other slide content. They allow you to keep text on a slide to a minimum, an important goal for a successful presentation.

Headers & Footers

Headers and footers are used to repeat information on every slide. For example, a date in the footer will be displayed in the footer area of every slide. PowerPoint uses footers for displaying information on slides; handouts and speaker notes contain both headers and footers.

To add repeating information to a presentation:

1. Click Insert ⇨ Header & Footer. A dialog box is displayed.
2. Click the details you want to be displayed on the slide. If you want custom footer text, click Footer and then type in the box.
3. *Optional*. Click Don't show on title slide if you don't want footers displayed on slides with the Title Slide layout (typically the first slide).
4. Click Apply if you want the footer information on the current slide only. Click Apply to All to add the information to all slides.

Header and footer information added to speaker notes and handouts pages will appear on printouts. To add headers or footers to notes and handouts pages:

1. Click Insert ⇨ Header & Footer. A dialog box is displayed.
2. Click the Notes and Handouts tab.
3. Click the details you want to be displayed on the pages. For custom text, click Header and/or Footer and then type text.
4. Click Apply to All to display the information on all the notes and handouts pages.

TIP The Date & Time and Slide Number commands on the Insert tab also display the Header and Footer dialog box when there are no objects selected on a slide.

TIP To add a single occurrence of the date and time or slide number, place the insertion point at the desired location in a content placeholder before you click Insert ⇨ Date & Time or Insert ⇨ Slide Number.

Changing the Slide Order

As your presentation develops, you may find that slides need to be reorganized. This can be done from three different presentation views:

- Normal View displays thumbnails that can dragged up or down to a new location.
- Outline View displays tiny slide icons along with title and main text. Drag an icon up or down to move a slide. You can also drag selected text to move it from one slide to another or to a different position within the same slide.
- Slide Sorter displays thumbnails that can be dragged to a new location in the presentation.

To change the order of slides:

1. Click the View tab and then click Normal, Outline View, or Slide Sorter in the Presentation Views group.

   Or

   Click the Normal or Slide Sorter button in the status bar.

2. Drag thumbnails or icons to change the order of the slides.

Review Your Presentation

When you're ready to get an idea of how your presentation will appear to an audience, switch to Reading View. In this view, you can play your slide show presentation in the PowerPoint window.

To play your presentation in Reading View:

1. Click View ⇨ Reading View or click   in the status bar. The first slide of your presentation is displayed in the full PowerPoint window.
2. Click the mouse button or use another method described in Table 5, p. 30 to proceed through the slide show.

   Or

   Click Previous   , Next   , or Menu   in the status bar.
3. End the slide show at any time by pressing the Esc key.

TIP To see how your presentation will convert to grayscale or black and white when printed, click a command in the Color/Grayscale group on the View tab.

TIP Play a slide show full screen by clicking Slide Show ⇨ From Beginning or Slide Show ⇨ From Current Slide. Refer to Chapter 6 "Delivering a Presentation" for more information.

Table 5 Reading View Keyboard Shortcuts

Perform the next animation or advance to the next slide	spacebar, N, Enter, down arrow, right arrow, PgDn
Perform the previous animation or return to the previous slide	Backspace, P, up arrow, left arrow, PgUp
Display the All Slides dialog box	Press Ctrl+S to display a dialog box where you can select the slide to go to.
End the slide show	Esc

Chapter 3
Presentation Design

Presentation design refers to the overall look of your slide show. Since a slide show is in effect another form of branding, you'll want to carefully consider the design. For example, one form of branding involves using the theme associated with your company when doing a presentation for your organization.

Using Themes

A *theme* is a named set of fonts, colors, slide background, and effects that provide a consistent look from one slide layout to another. PowerPoint has many built-in themes to choose from. The default theme is named Office Theme. You can use any theme as is or as the foundation for creating your own brand.

To apply a theme to your presentation:

1. Click Design ⇨ ▼ in the Themes group (Figure 24).

   Figure 24 The More button in the Themes group.

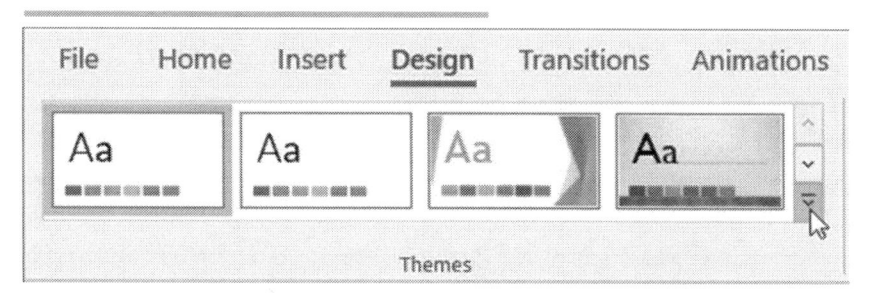

   A gallery is displayed. Point to a theme for a preview. Drag the scroll bar on the right of the gallery to view additional themes.

2. Click a theme to apply it.

3. *Optional*. After applying a theme, click a variation on the theme in the Variants group.

   Or

   Click More ▼ in the Variants group and use the menu of commands to change specific features of the selected theme.

4. *Optional*. Click Design ⇨ Format Background. The Format Background task pane with fill settings is opened. Changing the settings affects the current slide only. Click Apply to All in the task pane to apply the settings to all slide layouts in the theme.

5. *Optional*. Click Design ⇨ ▽ in the Themes group and then click Save Current Theme to save the modified theme with a descriptive name. The saved theme will be available for use in future presentations.

To apply a theme or variant to selected slides only:

1. Select the slides to receive the theme. (Table 6 below).

2. Click Design ⇨ ▽ in the Themes group. A gallery is displayed. Point to a theme for a preview. Drag the scroll bar on the right of the gallery to see additional themes.

3. Right-click a theme and select Add to Selected Slides. Or, click Add to Matching Slides to apply the theme to all slides with the same layout as the selected slide.

4. *Optional*. Right-click a variant and select Add to Selected Slides. Or, click Add to Matching Slides to apply the variant to all slides with the same layout as the selected slide.

TIP Office 365 subscribers may also have the Design Ideas button on the Design tab. Click this button and turn on Intelligent Services to allow PowerPoint to make design suggestions.

Table 6 Selecting Slides

Select a single slide	Click a thumbnail or use the arrow keys to select a thumbnail.
Select a range of slides	Click the first thumbnail in the range and then press and hold Shift before clicking the last thumbnail for the range.
Select multiple slides	Press and hold Ctrl while clicking thumbnails. This method allows noncontiguous slide selection.
Select all slides	Click a thumbnail and then click Home ⇨ Select ⇨ Select All.

Slide Master View

Themes are built from a slide master and a set of related layouts. In Slide Master View, you can modify the theme slide master, create new layouts, and add content to layouts that cannot be removed or changed from Normal View — ideal for adding logos and other branding to slides.

To modify a theme in Slide Master view:

1. Click View ⇨ Slide Master. Note the theme Slide Master is the very top thumbnail (Figure 25). You may have to scroll up to bring it into view. Thumbnails below the Slide Master are layout masters. Point to a thumbnail for a ScreenTip.

Figure 25 A Slide Master.

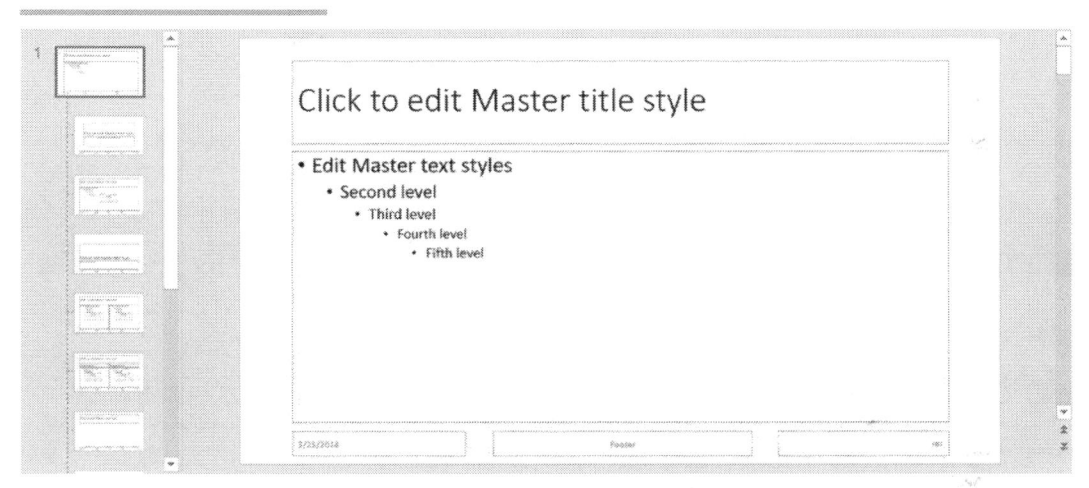

2. If you want to make global changes that affect the entire presentation, first click the Slide Master (the very top thumbnail). Some of the ways you can edit the Slide Master are:
    - Move, size, and delete placeholders. Or insert a new placeholder (Table 7, p. 34). This will affect layouts with similar placeholders.
    - Move, size, delete, and add graphic elements. Graphics are discussed in Chapter 4.
    - Click Slide Master ⇨ Themes to change or add a built-in theme (Table 7, p. 34).
    - Click Slide Master ⇨ Rename to change the name of the theme for the presentation (Table 7, p. 34).

Microsoft PowerPoint 2019 in 90 pages 34

3. Other global changes can be made with any thumbnail selected:
   - Click Colors, Fonts, or Effects in the Background group (Table 7 below).
   - Click Background Styles ⇨ Format Background (Table 7 below).
4. If you want to make changes to a specific layout, first click the desired layout. Some of the ways you can edit a layout are:
   - Move, size, and delete placeholders.
   - Insert new placeholders (Table 7 below).
   - Select a placeholder and then use commands on the Home and Shape Format tabs to make changes (do not use the global commands on the Slide Master tab.)
   - Click Background Styles (Table 7 below).
5. If you want a completely new, customizable layout for the theme, click Slide Master ⇨ Insert Layout. After inserting the layout, click Slide Master ⇨ Rename to give it a descriptive name (Table 7 below).
6. Click Slide Master ⇨ Close Master View to return to your presentation.

TIP After editing a layout in Slide Master, you must reapply the layout to an existing slide (Home ⇨ Layout).

TIP Click View ⇨ Handouts Master to customize printed handouts.

TIP Click View ⇨ Notes Master to customize speaker notes.

Figure 26 The Slide Master tab.

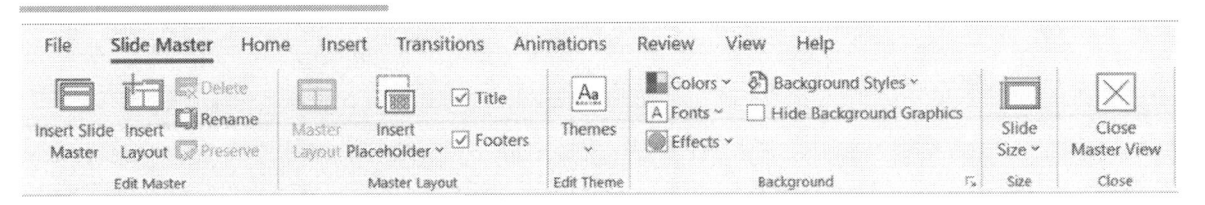

Table 7 Slide Master Tab

Insert Slide Master	Click to insert a custom design Slide Master set to the presentation.
Insert Layout	Click to add a new, customizable layout to the slide set.

Chapter 3 Presentation Design

Delete	Click to remove a Slide Master and its layouts. This command is available when there is more than one theme in Slide Master View.
Rename	Click a layout and then click Rename to give the layout a new name. Or, click the Slide Master and then click Rename to give the theme a new name.
Preserve	Click a Slide Master and then click Preserve to keep the theme with the presentation even if it is not used.
Master Layout	Click to display a dialog box for choosing the elements for the slide master.
Insert Placeholder	Click to add a placeholder to a slide layout. Click the Insert Placeholder arrow ⌄ to choose the type of placeholder to add. After clicking a type, draw the placeholder on the slide layout (the mouse pointer will be a crosshairs).
Title and Footers	Click a checkbox to add or remove an element from a slide layout.
Themes	Click to apply a theme to the Slide Master set. Right-click and then select Add a New Slide Master to add the theme's Slide Master set to the presentation.
Colors, Fonts, Effects	Selecting an option from these commands applies the change to the entire Slide Master set regardless of which Slide Master or layout is selected. Click the Custom command at the bottom of the Colors and Fonts menus to define your own set.
Background Styles	Click to change the current slide background. Click Background Styles ⇨ Format Background to open a task pane with Apply to All for changing a background for the entire slide set.
Hide Background Graphics	Click to hide the background graphics on the current slide.
Slide Size	Click for commands to change the current slide size. Refer to p. 12.

Transitions

After applying an overall design by using themes and the Slide Master, there are individual slide design considerations. A *transition* uses a special effect to remove one slide and display the next. For example, the Curtains transition dramatically reveals the next slide by making the previous slide appear like opening curtains, as in Figure 27.

Figure 27 A transition reveals the next slide by using a special effect.

To apply transitions to slides:

1. Click the thumbnail of the slide to receive the transition. (But keep in mind a transition determines how the previous slide exits the presentation.) If you want to apply a transition to multiple slides, first select the thumbnails (Table 6, p. 32).
2. Click the Transitions tab for the Transition to This Slide group.
3. Click a transition. A preview of the effect is played.

    Or

    Click More . A gallery is displayed. Click a transition. A preview is played.
4. *Optional.* Click Transitions ⇨ Effect Options if it is available and choose a variation for the selected transition.

5. *Optional*. Click Transitions ⇨ Apply To All to apply the transition to the entire slide show. It is good design to keep transitions consistent to avoid a slide show that comes off as confusing and distracting.

6. *Optional*. Change settings in the Timing group:

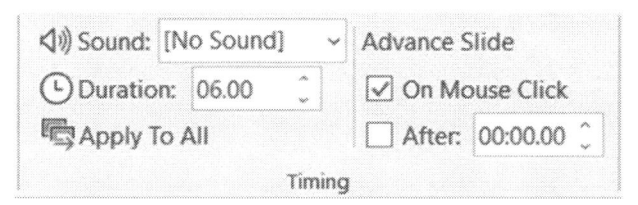

Sound: [No Sound]	Advance Slide
Duration: 06.00	☑ On Mouse Click
Apply To All	☐ After: 00:00.00

   Timing

   - Click the Sound arrow and select a sound effect. This type of effect can be distracting, so use with careful consideration.
   - Duration refers to the length of the transition. Type a time in seconds or use the arrow buttons to change the duration.
   - Clear the On Mouse Click checkbox, click the After box, and type an advance time in seconds in the After box when you want to automate a slide show. (Refer to TIP on p. 81.)
   - Click Apply To All to apply timing settings to the entire slide show.

7. If you want to remove a transition, select a thumbnail and click Transitions ⇨ None from the gallery.

TIP Click the Animations icon next to a thumbnail in Normal view to preview its transition.

TIP Transitions can be added to Slide Master View.

The Morph Transition

The *Morph transition* is an effect that creates a smooth movement from one slide to the next. Because the transition animates objects between slides, Morph can be applied only to slides where at least one object is duplicated and repositioned and/or resized on the second slide.

Morph will not transform an object from say a lion to a kitten. But you can transform a shape to one that has been formatted with a different position, size, color, outline, and so on. When transitioning from one slide to the next, the audience sees only a smooth morphing of objects. This transition is very effective when you want your presentation to have a movie-like feel.

To get a better idea of how Morph works, consider a fictional Happy Pet Vet presentation. Happy Pet runs the slide show continuously in the waiting area to remind clients of their services. Figure 28 shows the first four slides. When slide 1 transitions to slide 2, the dog will appear to "grow" and move into position. From slide 2 to slide 3, the dog "shrinks" as the cat "grows" into position, and finally, in slide 4, the small mammal "grows" into position while the cat "shrinks" back down.

Figure 28 Morph transition requires at least one duplicate item between slides.

To use the Morph transition:

1. Create a slide with text and/or objects.

2. With the slide created in step 1 displayed in Normal view, click Home ⇨ New Slide ⇨ Duplicate Selected Slides. A duplicate of the slide created in step 1 is displayed.

3. Make changes to the duplicate slide, keeping in mind that Morph requires you keep at least one object from the previous slide. You can delete objects and text, resize and move objects, change font size and color for text, apply or change WordArt effects to text, and so on.

4. Click Transitions ⇨ Morph. A preview of the effect is played. Text and objects that were added to the slide fade in, text and objects that were deleted fade out, modified text and objects morph into their new formats and shapes.

5. Refer to Steps 4 through 7 in "Transitions" above to make optional modifications to the transition.

TIP Click the Animations icon ★ next to a thumbnail in Normal view to preview the slide's transition.

Animations

Within a slide, *animations* get the attention of your audience through action. For example, during a presentation you can keep your bullet points hidden until you trigger their display, usually by a click of the mouse. The trigger uses the assigned animation, such as Fly In, to bring a bullet point onto the slide.

Animations are grouped into Entrance, Emphasis, Exit, and Motion Paths. Besides bullet points of text, animations can be applied to graphics, text boxes, and other objects. In Figure 29, the dog icon has been assigned a motion path animation. The dotted line indicates the path the object will move along when the animation is triggered on the fifth mouse click.

Figure 29 The fifth animation is a motion path.

How to Reward Your Dog

1. • A good belly rub
2. • A pat on the head
3. • A small treat
4. • Kind words in a loving tone of voice
5.

To apply animations to bullet points and objects:

1. Click in a bulleted or numbered list.

   Or

   Click an object to select it. Handles will be displayed.

2. Click the Animations tab.

3. Click More ⏷ in the Animation group. A gallery is displayed. Animations are divided into Entrance, Emphasis, Exit, and Motion Paths (you may need to scroll to see them all). Click an animation from the appropriate group, depending on when you want the animation triggered. A preview is played and a number(s) displayed to indicate which mouse click will trigger the animation.

4. *Optional.* Click Animations ⇨ Effect Options if it is available and choose a variation for the selected animation.

5. *Optional.* Click Animations ⇨ Add Animation to select an additional transition for the text or object. For example, you can choose an Exit animation in addition to the Entrance animation. However, you should consider the impact on your audience before adding even more action to your slide.

6. *Optional.* The default trigger for an animation is a random mouse click. However, you can change the trigger to relate to a specified object. To do this, click Animations ⇨ Trigger ⇨ On Click of and select an object. (To clear the trigger, click Trigger ⇨ On Click of and clear the check box next to the trigger object.)

7. *Optional.* Change settings in the Timing group:

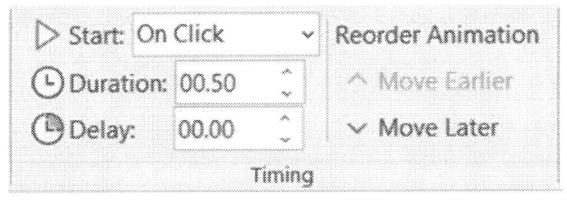

   - Click the Start arrow and select an animation trigger. To automate timings, select After Previous and set a Duration.
   - Duration refers to the length of the animation. Type a time in seconds or use the arrow buttons to change the duration.
   - If you want the animation to start after the trigger, change the Delay time.
   - Click the Reorder Animation arrows to change the order of animation groups.

8. To animate additional objects, repeat steps 1 through 7.
9. *Optional*. Click Animations ⇨ Animation Pane. A pane with all the applied animations and their settings is opened (Figure 30).

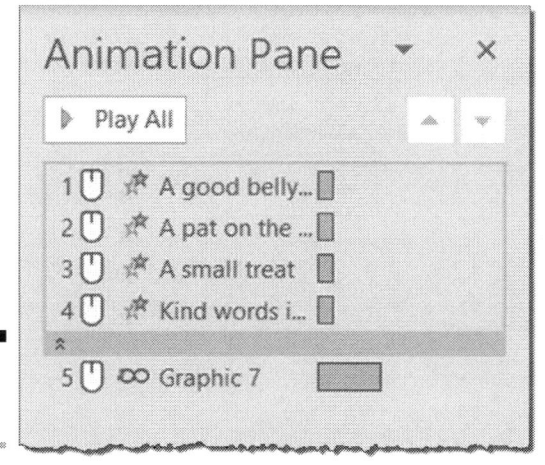

Figure 30 Animation task pane.

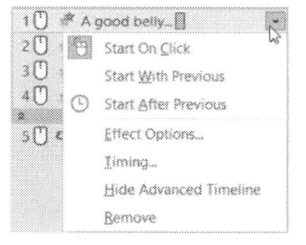

- Click an animation and then click the displayed arrow for a menu with Effect Options and Timings commands. Click a command for advanced settings, including sound effects.
- Drag animations up or down to change the trigger order.
- Drag the edge of a timeline icon to edit the duration: 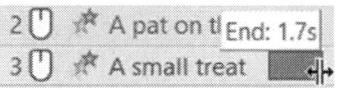
- Drag the entire icon to edit the delay:

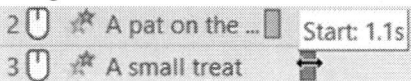

10. If you want to remove an animation, click Animations ⇨ None from the gallery or delete the animation from the Animation pane.

TIP Click the Animations icon next to a thumbnail in Normal view to preview the slide's animations.

TIP Animations may interfere with the desired effect of a Morph transition.

TIP You can also use a video or audio clip bookmark (Chapter 4) as the animation trigger for a bullet point or object. Click Animations ⇨ Trigger ⇨ On Bookmark and select a bookmark.

Tables

How to display data is another important aspect of presentation design. One approach is to use tables, which organize information into rows and columns that are formatted for easier reading (Figure 31). The intersection of a row and column is called a *cell*.

Figure 31 A table makes data easier to comprehend.

Breed	Weight
Boston Terrier	10 – 25 lb. (4.5 – 11 kg.)
Basset Hound	40 – 60 lb. (18 – 27 kg.)
Labrador Retriever	65 – 80 lb. (29 – 36 kg.)

To add a table to a slide:

1. Click Insert ⇨ Table and then move the pointer around the grid without clicking for a preview. Click when you have the desired grid highlighted. A table is added to the slide.

    Or

    Click Insert ⇨ Table ⇨ Insert Table. A dialog box is displayed. Type the Number of columns and the Number of rows and then select OK. A table is added to the slide.

2. Enter data for the table by clicking in a cell and typing. Press the Tab key to move from cell to cell or use the mouse to click in a cell.

Chapter 3 Presentation Design

3. *Optional.* Tables are *floating* objects. Point to the edge of the table until the four-headed move pointer is displayed and then drag the table to the desired location on the slide.
4. *Optional.* Use Table Design tab commands (Table 8, p. 43) to change the overall look of the table and to format individual cells.
5. *Optional.* Use Layout tab commands (Table 9, p. 45) to change the table structure.
6. *Optional.* To format text in individual cells, click in the desired cell and then use commands on the Home tab. To format specific text within a cell, first select only the text to format and then use commands on the Home tab.
7. *Optional.* To apply text formats to the entire table at once, first select Layout ⇨ Select ⇨ Select Table and then use commands on the Home tab or on the Table Design tab in the WordArt group. (The Select command will be unavailable if the table is already selected.)

TIP Click Insert ⇨ Table ⇨ Draw Table and then drag the pencil pointer on the slide to create a custom table.

TIP Click Insert ⇨ Table ⇨ Excel Spreadsheet when you need a table that can include functions, formulas, and other spreadsheet features.

TIP To insert an existing table from a Word document, in Word click the Table Move Handle, click Home ⇨ Copy, switch to the PowerPoint slide, and click the Home ⇨ Paste arrow and select a Paste Special option.

Table 8 Table Design Tab

Table Style Options group	Click a checkbox to emphasize rows and columns.
Table Styles	Click More in the Table Styles group for a gallery of styles. Point to a style to preview the effect. Click a style to apply it.

Shading		Click the Shading button to change the background of the current cell. If you want to repeat formats across every cell, first select Layout ⇨ Select ⇨ Select Table. (The Select command will be unavailable if the table is already selected.)
		Click Shading ⇨ Table Background to use a picture or texture for the entire table background. *You will need to click Shading ⇨ No Fill for the entire table for the background to be visible.
Borders		Click the Borders arrow to add or remove borders for the current cell. If you want to apply border formats to the entire table, first select Layout ⇨ Select ⇨ Select Table. (The Select command will be unavailable if the table is already selected.)
Effects		Click the Effects arrow to add or remove effects for the current cell. If you want to apply effects to the entire table, first select Layout ⇨ Select ⇨ Select Table. (The Select command will be unavailable if the table is already selected.)
WordArt Styles group		Contains commands to format text in the current cell with fill patterns, outlines, and effects. If you want to apply WordArt to the entire table, first select Layout ⇨ Select ⇨ Select Table. (The Select command will be unavailable if the table is already selected.) Refer to Chapter 2, p. 22 for more information on WordArt.
Draw Borders group		Select an option from the Pen Color, Pen Style, and/or Pen Weight, and click a table border to apply the settings. Press Esc to end the edits. You can also draw a table inside a cell or on the slide when the pencil pointer is displayed. Click Eraser and then click a border to remove it.

Table 9 Layout tab

Select	Click for a menu of options to select part or all of a table relative to the cell containing the insertion point. You can also select a cell by pointing inside the left edge and clicking the ↗ pointer. To select a column, point above the column and click the ↓ pointer. To select a row, point to the left of a row and the click the ➡ pointer. To select an entire table, point to a table edge and click the four-headed arrow ✥ pointer.
View Gridlines	Click to display non-printing gridlines.
Delete	Click for a menu of options to delete columns, rows, or table.
Rows & Columns group	Contains commands to add and remove rows and columns relative to the active cell.
Merge group	Contains commands to merge and split cells. To merge adjacent cells into one, you first drag the insertion point from one cell to the last in the group to be merged and then click Merge Cells. You can also click Table Design ⇨ Eraser and then click a border to automatically merge cells.
Cell Size group	Type values in the Height and Width boxes or click the arrows to adjust row and column sizes. You can also point to the row or column border and then drag the double-headed arrow pointer. Double-click a row or column border to get a best fit size based on your content.
Alignment group	Click options to set alignment and text direction for selected cells. Click Cell Margins ⇨ Custom Margins for a dialog box to set cell margins (the space between the cell contents and the cell borders) for the entire table.
Table Size group	Click options to change the overall table size. Click Lock Aspect Ratio to maintain the proportions when sizing.
Arrange group	Refer to Table 12 Arranging Multiple Objects on p. 51.

Sections

A presentation can be divided into named *sections* that group related slides. The audience won't be aware of the sections, but from a design standpoint, they organize presentation development. Sections are especially helpful when you want to assign portions of a presentation to collaborators (Chapter 7).

To divide a presentation into sections:

1. Click the thumbnail that is to begin a new section.

   Or

   Click just below a thumbnail. A thin line is displayed.
2. Click Home ⇨ Section ⇨ Add Section. A dialog box is displayed.
3. Type a name for the section and click OK. The section name is displayed with a triangle icon, which can be clicked to collapse or expand the thumbnails associated with the section.
4. If you want to reorder slides, drag a section name to move the entire section of slides.
5. If you want to add a slide to a section, click in the section to display a thin line and then click Home ⇨ New Slide and select the desired slide layout.
6. Use the commands in Home ⇨ Section to rename, delete, collapse, and expand sections.

Zoom for Nonlinear Navigation

Use the Insert ⇨ Zoom commands to create a presentation that allows you to navigate slides in a nonlinear fashion.

To add Zoom capabilities to your presentation:

1. Click Insert ⇨ Zoom ⇨ Slide Zoom, click slide(s), and click Insert. The selected slides appear as thumbnail sized image(s) on the current slide. During a presentation, click a thumbnail to zoom to that slide; click again to zoom back to the current slide. Insert ⇨ Zoom ⇨ Section Zoom works similarly.
2. Click Insert ⇨ Zoom ⇨ Summary Zoom, click the slides that you want to be on a summary slide, and then click Insert. A new slide is created with thumbnails to the slides so that you can zoom back and forth between them.

Chapter 4
Graphics, Video, and Audio

Audiences pay attention to graphics, video, and audio which can increase comprehension and content retention. Give your slides more impact through pictures, 3-D models, text boxes, shapes, SmartArt, and media files.

Pictures

Company logos and other images make a presentation more interesting and are important for reinforcing your brand with the audience.

To add an image to the current slide:

1. If your slide layout includes content placeholders, click in a placeholder. When inserted, your image will automatically size to fit the placeholder.

   Or

   Click outside any placeholders so that nothing is selected on the slide. This step will allow you to later drag the inserted picture to any position on the slide.

2. Click Insert ⇨ Pictures to add an image from one of your storage devices. A dialog box is displayed.

   Or

   Click Insert ⇨ Online Pictures to search the Internet. A dialog box is displayed.

3. Navigate to the appropriate location and select the image. Images can be in one of many formats, commonly JPEG, TIF, or GIF.

   Or

   If you're inserting an online picture, type a search word to begin the process of finding a relevant image. (Copyright protects images on the Internet. Click the Creative Commons licenses link in the dialog box for more information.)

   The inserted image displays sizing handles and a rotation handle. In Figure 32, p. 48, the slide layout is Content with Caption and the insertion point was in the content placeholder.

Figure 32 A selected picture displays sizing handles and a rotation handle.

4. *Optional.* Size or rotate the image as desired (Table 10, p. 49).
5. *Optional.* Crop the image as desired (Table 11, p. 49).
6. *Optional.* Pictures and other graphics are *floating* objects. Drag the image to the desired location on the slide (Table 10, p. 49).
7. *Optional.* Use Picture Format tab commands (Table 11, p. 49) to adjust the image color or change the picture styles, border, and effects. If necessary, first click the picture to select it.
8. *Optional.* Use the Animations tab to apply an animation (p. 39) to a selected picture.

TIP When you want an image at the same location on every slide, add the image to the appropriate master in Slide Master view.

TIP Click Insert ⇨ Screenshot to insert a screenshot from a currently open application window. Click Insert ⇨ Screenshot ⇨ Screen Clipping to insert part of an active screen.

TIP A very large image may greatly increase your file size. If this is an issue, when selecting the image file, click the Insert arrow ⌄ in the Insert Picture dialog box and select Link to File.

Chapter 4 Graphics, Video, and Audio

Table 10 Object Editing

Size	Drag a sizing handle (the circles displayed around a selected object).
	Press and hold the Shift key while you drag a corner handle to maintain the aspect ratio.
	If you want the center of the image to remain in place while sizing, then press and hold Ctrl+Shift while dragging a corner handle.
	When you want the image to fill the slide, you can drag the size handles, which gives you more control over how the image is placed on the slide. Alternatively, click Design ⇨ Format Background and to open the Format Background task pane and then use the Fill option to select a background picture.
Rotate	Drag the circular rotation handle (object must be selected).
Move	Point to an object and then drag with the four-headed arrow pointer to reposition. Smart guides are displayed as the object moves to help with placement.
Right-click	Right-click an object for a menu of commands for formatting, editing alt text, and controlling object-specific features.

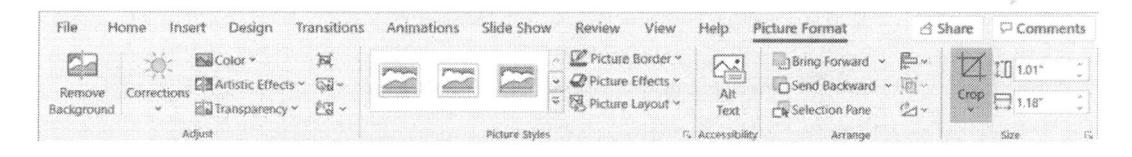

Table 11 Picture Format Tab

(Click a picture to make this tab available)

Remove Background	Click to have PowerPoint make a best guess at the picture background. The command displays the Background Removal tab with options for further specifying which part of an image should be removed.

Microsoft PowerPoint 2019 in 90 pages — 50

Corrections	Click for options to sharpen an image and improve contrast.
Color	Click for options to correct or recolor an image.
Artistic Effects	Click to change the look of an image.
Transparency	Click for transparency options for an image. *If you don't have this command, insert a picture into a text box and then adjust the text box transparency. Follow steps 1, 2, 4, 5 on p. 52.
Compress Pictures	Click for a dialog box of options for reducing image sizes. File size is a consideration when emailing a presentation.
Change Picture	Click to switch the picture with a different one.
Reset Picture	Click to remove all formats.
Picture Styles group	Click a predefined style to change the look of your picture. Click More to see the complete gallery of styles. Click Picture Border, Picture Effects, and Picture Layout for more options.
Alt Text	Click to open the Alt Text pane to type a picture description for screen readers.
Arrange Group	Refer to Table 12, p. 51.
Rotate	Click for precise rotation options.
Crop	Click to display cropping handles (solid black lines). Drag the handles to exclude portions of your photo. Click outside the photo after you define the crop area. (The bottom crop handle has been dragged up in the image to the left.) Click the Crop button arrow for a menu of commands. Crop to Shape allows you to choose a shape for your image.
Height, Width	Click in the Height or Width boxes and type an exact size. When a size is entered for one dimension, the other changes proportionately.
Size group	Click for more size options.

Arranging Objects

To help you align or otherwise arrange objects on your slides, use commands on the Picture Format, Shape Format, or View tabs. You may also click Home ⇨ Arrange ⇨ Selection Pane for a list of objects on the slide.

Table 12 Arranging Multiple Objects

Picture Format and Shape Format tabs Arrange group

Selection Pane	Click to display a list of objects for the current slide. You can click an object in the list to select it on the slide. When a graphic is hidden behind another, this is one way to select it.
Align	Click to display a menu of options for aligning one or more selected objects. To select multiple objects together, click the first object, and then press and hold the Ctrl key while you click additional objects.
Bring Forward, Send Backward	Click to bring a selected object to the front of overlapping objects or send to the back of overlapping objects.
Group	Click to join two or more selected objects together. Grouped objects can be moved and formatted as a single object.

View tab Show group

Ruler	Click to display vertical and horizontal rulers in the Slide pane.
Gridlines	Click to display a non-printing gridline on the slide.
Guides	Click to display guides on a slide. Right-click a slide and point to the arrow for the Grid and Guides command for Add Vertical Guide and Add Horizontal Guide commands. Drag a guide to reposition it. Guides can be added to a slide master.
Show group dialog box launcher	Click to display the Grid and Guides dialog box.

Text Boxes

Text boxes are containers for text and pictures.

To add a text box to the current slide:

1. Click Insert ⇨ Text Box. The pointer changes to ↓ when moved onto the slide.
2. Drag the pointer where you want the text box. The created text box displays a blinking insertion point.
3. Type your text and then apply formats using commands on the Home tab in the Font group (Table 13, pp. 53 – 54).
4. *Optional.* Use Shape Format ⇨ Shape Fill to change the text box background to include a picture, gradient, or texture. This can be done with or without text in the box.
5. *Optional.* On the Shape Format tab, click ⬒ in the Shape Styles group to open the Format Shape task pane with additional formatting options, including the Transparency option (under the Fill options). (Figure 33 and Table 13, pp. 53 – 54.)

Figure 33 The text box has a solid fill with 33% transparency.

Chapter 4 Graphics, Video, and Audio

6. *Optional.* Size or rotate the text box as desired (Table 10, p. 49).
7. *Optional.* Drag the text box to the desired location on the slide (Table 10, p. 49). You may need to drag the edge, not the center of the text box.
8. *Optional.* Use the Animations tab to apply an animation (p. 39) to a selected textbox.

WordArt Text Boxes

From the Insert tab, you can create a WordArt object with all the same properties of a text box.

To add a WordArt object to the current slide:

1. Click Insert ⇨ WordArt and then pick the style you want. A WordArt text box is added to the slide.
2. Type your text. If typing does not replace the text in the box, be sure that the existing text has been selected before typing. You may need to drag a handle to resize the text box to accommodate text.
3. *Optional.* Use commands on the Shape Format tab to format the text box (Table 13, below) and change the WordArt styles.
4. *Optional.* Refer to steps 4 through 8 above to further edit your WordArt text box.

Table 13 Shape Format Tab

Edit Shape	Click to change the shape or display points that can be dragged to create a customized shape.
Merge Shapes	Click to combine multiple selected shapes into one. (Press the Ctrl key and click each shape.)
Shape Styles group	Click a predefined style to change the look of your shape. Click More to see the complete gallery of styles. Click Shape Fill, Shape Outline, and Shape Effects for more options.
Transparency	Click to open the Format Shape task pane. Click Fill & Line and then expand the Fill group to make the Transparency option available.

WordArt Styles group	WordArt styles can be applied to text in a shape. Refer to Chapter 2, p. 22.
Arrange group	Refer to Table 10, p. 49 and Table 12, p. 51.
Size group	Refer to Table 11, p. 49.

Shapes

You can draw shapes, such as lines, arrows, and banners, onto your slides. Many shapes also support text, as with the banner in Figure 34.

Figure 34 The banner shape can include text.

To add a shape to the current slide:

1. Click Insert ⇨ Shapes and then click the shape you want. You may need to scroll the menu to see the entire list. The pointer changes to crosshairs when moved onto the slide.
2. Drag the pointer where you want the shape.

3. If the shape you've added supports text, double-click the center of the shape to display the insertion point, type the text for your shape, and then apply formats using commands on the Home tab in the Font group or WordArt commands on the Shape Format tab (Table 13, pp. 53 – 54). If you are typing a lot of text, you may need to make the shape larger.
4. *Optional*. Size or rotate the shape as desired (Table 10, p. 49).
5. *Optional*. Drag the shape to the desired location on the slide (Table 10, p. 49).
6. *Optional*. Use the Shape Format tab to customize your shape. Click ⌐ in the Shape Styles group to change the background and transparency of the shape. Refer to Table 13, pp. 53 – 54.
7. *Optional*. Use the Animations tab to apply an animation (p. 39).

TIP Refer to "Action Objects" later in this chapter to learn how to use the Action Buttons shapes.

TIP Click Insert ⇨ Icons to add symbols that communicate ideas. Icons are Scalable Vector Graphics (SVGs) that can be sized (scaled) without losing quality.

3D Models

3-D models are an exciting way to add impact to your presentation. Imagine a prospective client seeing your product in 3D.

To add a 3D model to the current slide:

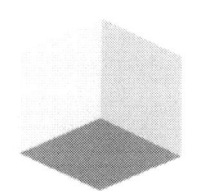

1. Click Insert ⇨ 3D Models. You can insert a model from a file or choose one online. (You can create your own models using Microsoft Paint 3D.)
2. You can size and move the model like you would a picture. Change the angle of view by dragging the rotation handle ⊕.
3. *Optional*. Use the Animations tab to apply a 3D animation.
4. *Optional*. Use the Morph transition to animate your 3D model. PowerPoint will use the aspects of your 3D model to morph an object to a new position and view. For example, a block on one slide will appear to tumble when morphed to the next slide where the block has been placed in a lower position in a different view. Be sure there are no animations on the slides that are morphed.

SmartArt

SmartArt graphics visually convey ideas ranging from the sequence in a cycle to organizational charts to a family tree. They often incorporate images along with text and graphics and offer a creative, quick way to present information in an eye-catching format. You can even convert a bulleted list to a SmartArt graphic.

To add SmartArt objects to a displayed slide:

1. Click Insert ➪ SmartArt. A dialog box is displayed (Figure 35).

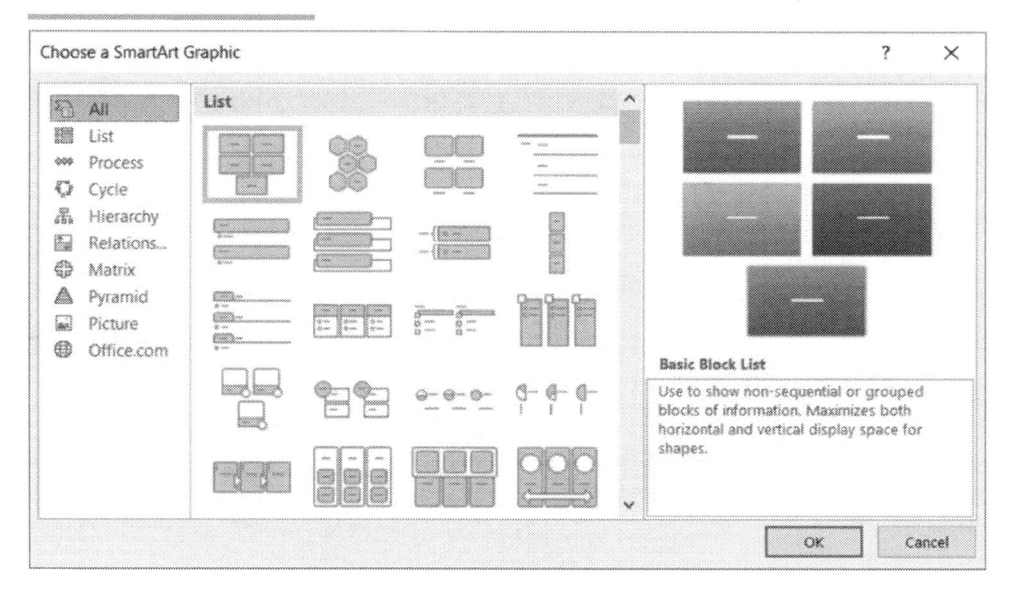

Figure 35 The SmartArt dialog box.

2. Choose a SmartArt graphic and click OK. You can first narrow the list by clicking a group name on the left side of the dialog box. The SmartArt graphic is added as a floating object.
3. A SmartArt graphic displays text boxes where you need text, and photo icons where you need images. Click a text box to enter your own text. Click a photo icon to display a dialog box where you can navigate to an image.
4. *Optional.* Click SmartArt Design ➪ Text Pane. A text pane is displayed where you can enter text for your SmartArt.
5. *Optional.* If you need to extend your SmartArt, use commands on the SmartArt Design tab in the Create Graphic group. To reduce the SmartArt, delete bullets in the text pane.

6. *Optional.* To move your SmartArt, drag the edge of the object, not the center where the objects are. You can size the object by dragging a sizing handle. Change the angle of the graphic by dragging the circular rotation handle.

7. *Optional.* SmartArt is a collection of shapes. Right-click an individual shape and then click Change Shape for shape options or click Add Shape to extend the SmartArt graphic. Use the handles on selected shapes to rotate or size individual shapes.

8. *Optional.* Use commands on the SmartArt Design tab to choose layout and style options. To format individual shapes, use commands on the Format tab.

9. *Optional.* Use the Animations tab to apply an animation (p. 39) to a selected SmartArt or object within the SmartArt.

To convert a bulleted list to a SmartArt object:

1. Right-click a bulleted list and then click Convert to SmartArt. A gallery of SmartArt options is displayed.

2. Point to an option for a preview. Click to covert text to SmartArt.

3. Refer to the steps above for customizing the SmartArt.

TIP Not all SmartArt graphics support animations for individual graphics. Therefore, converting a bulleted list to SmartArt may create one item rather than separate items that can have multiple animations applied.

Hyperlinks

Hyperlinks in a presentation can be used to open a web page, display a file, or take you to a different place in the presentation. Inserting an active web page link into a slide is as easy as typing it. PowerPoint interprets text such as @, .com, and www. as part of a hyperlink and automatically converts the text into a link. Plain text, shapes, and pictures can also be formatted as links.

To convert text or an object, such as a picture, to a hyperlink:

1. Select the text or click the object to convert to an active link.

2. Click Insert ⇨ Link ⇨ Insert Link to display a dialog box where you specify Link to information. You can choose to link to:

- Existing File or Web Page. You can select a location from the Look in list or type a URL in the Address box. Click 🔍 to open a browser so you can locate the page you want to link to and then copy and paste the URL to the Address box. Clicking the link during a presentation opens the document or web page in a corresponding application window.
- Place in This Document. You can select a slide in the presentation. Clicking the link during a presentation advances the slide show to the linked slide.
- Create New Document. You can enter the name of a new document that you can edit now or later. Clicking the link during a presentation displays the new document in a corresponding application window.
- E-mail Address. You can enter an email address and other information. Clicking the link during a presentation opens a new email for editing.
3. To edit an existing link, right-click the link and select Edit Link. The right-click menu also contains commands to Open Link, Copy Link, and Remove Link.

TIP Linking to images, files, and videos, rather than embedding them, can reduce the size of a PowerPoint file and reduce glitches during a presentation.

TIP Click Insert ⇨ Zoom ⇨ Slide Zoom to link to a slide (p. 46).

TIP When typed text is converted by mistake, click Undo on the Quick Access toolbar (Ctrl+Z) immediately after typing, or right-click the link and select Remove Link.

Action Objects

Shapes, pictures, and even text can be formatted as action objects that play a sound, start a program, or link to a slide or URL with a click or mouse over during a presentation. PowerPoint also includes a set of button shapes that have default actions associated with them.

To add an action to an object on the current slide:

1. Click an object or select text.
2. Click Insert ⇨ Action. A dialog box is displayed.
3. Click the Mouse Click tab or the Mouse Over tab.

Chapter 4 Graphics, Video, and Audio

4. Select the action to perform and other associated options from a list or Browse button.
5. *Optional.* Select special effects (Play sound and Highlight options).
6. Click OK.

To add an action button to the current slide:

1. Click Insert ⇨ Shapes and then select a shape from the Action Buttons group (Figure 36). Point to a shape for a description.

Figure 36 The bottom of the Shapes menu contains Action Buttons.

2. Move the pointer to the area where you want the shape and then drag to create it. A dialog box is displayed.
3. Modify action settings, if needed, and then select OK.
4. *Optional.* Format the shape as described in "Shapes" on p. 54.

Video

Video is often a favorite in presentations. A short video really grabs the audience's attention.

To add video to the current slide:

1. Click Insert ⇨ Video and then select Video on My PC. A dialog box is displayed so that you can insert a video from one of your storage devices.

   Or

   Click Insert ⇨ Video and then select Online Video. A dialog box is displayed so that you can enter the URL of a YouTube or Vimeo video.

2. For Video on My PC, navigate to the appropriate location on one of your storage devices and select a video. Videos in the MP4 format are recommended for PowerPoint. Controls below the inserted video can be used to preview the video.

   *During a presentation, point the mouse to the bottom of the video frame to display video controls.

Or

If you're inserting an online video:

- Open your web browser and locate the video.
- Copy the web page URL from the Address bar.
- Switch back to PowerPoint and paste the URL into the Online Video dialog and then click Insert.
- Click the Play button to preview the video.

*During a presentation, you will need to click the video frame. You will also need Internet access to connect to the video.

3. *Optional*. Use the Video Format tab commands to format the video frame (Table 14, p. 61).
4. *Optional*. Use the Playback tab commands to set video play options (Table 14, p. 61).
5. *Optional*. Click Animations ⇨ Animation Pane. In the Animation Pane, click the arrow next to the video object and select Effect Options for a dialog box with additional playback options.

TIP You can also create your own screen recording videos (Chapter 5).

TIP Refer to Chapter 6 for converting your entire presentation to a video.

Table 14 Video Tabs

Video Format Tab

Play	Click to play (preview) the video with applied formats in the PowerPoint window.
Corrections	Click for preset options and the Video Corrections Options command for displaying the Format Video pane.
Color	Click for color correction options.
Poster Frame	Used to change the preview frame for a video. Click the Play button below the video on the slide. When the desired frame is displayed, click Poster Frame ⇨ Current Frame.
Reset Design	Click to reverse all applied frame settings.

Chapter 4 Graphics, Video, and Audio

Video Styles group	Click More ⌵ in the Video Styles group for a gallery of frame styles. Point to a style to preview the effect. Click a style to apply it. Use the Video Shape, Video Border, and Video Effects options to further customize the frame.
Alt Text	Click to open the Alt Text pane to type a video description for screen readers.
Arrange group	Refer to Table 12, p. 51.
Size group	Refer to Table 11, p. 49.

Playback Tab
(Many commands work with videos on your PC only)

Play	Click to play (preview) the video with applied formats in the PowerPoint window.
Bookmarks group	Contains commands to mark or clear a position on the video timeline. Click the video Play button on the slide. When the desired frame is displayed, click Add Bookmark. A mark is added to the video timeline. During a presentation you need only click the bookmark to jump to that point in the video. Bookmarks can also be used to trigger an animation (refer to TIP on p. 41). To remove a bookmark, click the marker and click Remove Bookmark.
Trim Video	Click to display a dialog box where you can drag start and stop markers to trim the video length.
Fade Duration	Commands to change the Fade In and Fade Out times for a fade effect at the beginning or end of a video.
Volume	Click to select a volume level for video playback.

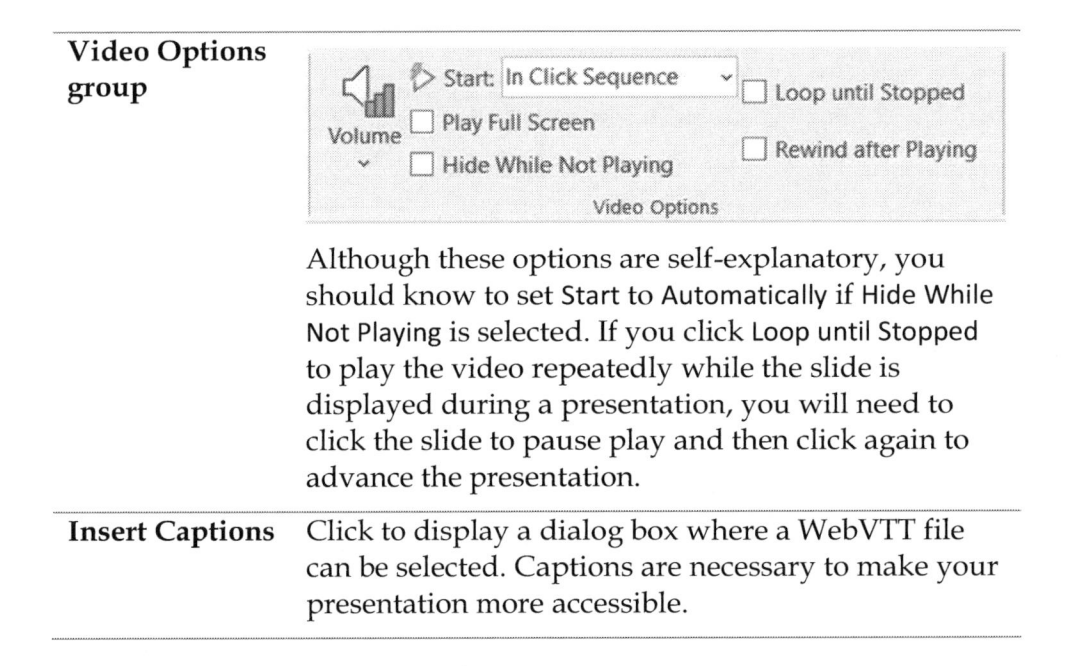

Video Options group	Although these options are self-explanatory, you should know to set Start to Automatically if Hide While Not Playing is selected. If you click Loop until Stopped to play the video repeatedly while the slide is displayed during a presentation, you will need to click the slide to pause play and then click again to advance the presentation.
Insert Captions	Click to display a dialog box where a WebVTT file can be selected. Captions are necessary to make your presentation more accessible.

Screen Recording Video

You can create your own custom screen recordings to insert as a video on a slide. Screen recordings are useful when you want to provide tutorials or other training related to a computer application.

To create and insert a screen recording:

1. Open the application window that you want to use for the recording.
2. Switch to your PowerPoint presentation and display the slide to receive the screen recording.
3. Click Insert ⇨ Screen Recording (in the Media group). The PowerPoint window is minimized, and the Control Dock is displayed (Figure 37, p. 63).

Chapter 4 Graphics, Video, and Audio 63

Figure 37 The screen recording Control Dock.

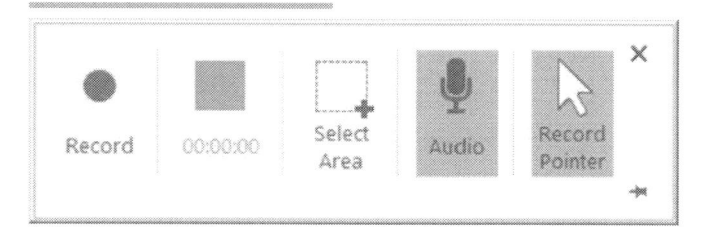

4. Click Select Area on the Control Dock (refer to Figure 37 above) and then drag on the screen to select the area to record. (Press the Windows logo key ⊞+Shift+F to record the entire screen.)
5. *Optional*. Click Audio on the Control Dock to toggle audio recording.
6. *Optional*. Click Record Pointer on the Control Dock to toggle the mouse pointer display during recording.
7. Click Record on the Control Dock to start recording. The Control Dock is hidden, and a countdown is displayed.
8. *Optional*. To pause recording, point the mouse to the top of the screen to display the Control Dock and then click the Pause button (Figure 38). When you are ready to record again, click Record. To end recording, click the X box to close the Control Dock.
9. To stop recording, point the mouse to the top of the screen to display the Control Dock and then click the Stop button (Figure 38 below).

Or

Stop the recording by pressing Windows logo key ⊞+Shift+Q.

Figure 38 The Control Dock Stop button appears like a square.

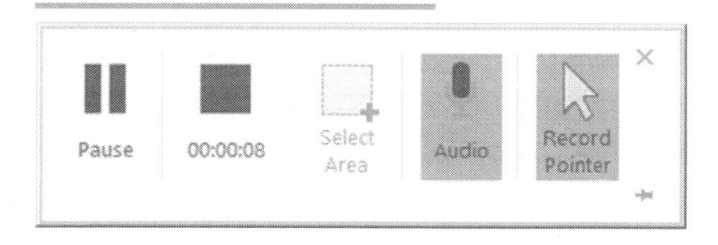

10. When you stop the recording, the video is added to the current slide (you may need to switch to the PowerPoint window). Use the Video Format and Playback tabs to format the video frame, control playback, and add captions (Table 14, p. 60 – 62).
11. *Optional.* Right-click the video object and select Save Media as to save the video as a separate video file.
12. *Optional.* Right-click the video object for related commands and a mini toolbar with Style, Trim, and Start buttons.

Audio

Audio refers to sound recordings such as music and narration, which can be played from just one slide or during the entire presentation. However, playing music throughout your presentation can be distracting. Exceptions include a photo album presentation (Chapter 5) or other type of presentation which does not require you to talk over the audio.

To add an audio clip to the current slide:

1. Click Insert ⇨ Audio ⇨ Audio on My PC (in the Media group). A dialog box is displayed.
2. Navigate to the desired audio file and then click Insert. An audio icon and controls are added to the slide (Figure 39).

Figure 39 The audio icon and controls.

3. Drag the icon to a convenient location on the slide.
4. If you want the audio file to play throughout a presentation, click Playback ⇨ Play in Background. Commands in the Audio Options group will be automatically set to continuously play the file throughout the presentation.

   *To manage background play, click Animations ⇨ Animation Pane. In the Animation Pane, click the arrow next to the audio object and select Effect Options for a dialog box where you can select when to start and stop the background audio, including which slides to play across.

Chapter 4 Graphics, Video, and Audio

Or

If you want to manually play the audio file from the slide, click Playback ⇨ No Style and then use the Playback tab commands to set options (Table 15, p. 66), if desired.

*During a presentation, point to the bottom of the icon to display audio controls.

5. *Optional.* Size and rotate the selected icon (Table 10, p. 49).

6. *Optional.* Use Audio Format tab commands (similar commands as in Table 11, p. 49) to adjust the icon color, styles, border, and effects. If necessary, first click the icon to select it.

To create your own audio clip and add it to the current slide:

1. Be sure your computer is equipped with a sound card, microphone, and speakers.

2. Click Insert ⇨ Audio ⇨ Record Audio. A dialog box is displayed.

3. Type a descriptive name and then click the Record button (Figure 40).

Figure 40 The Play, Stop, and Record controls (from left to right).

4. When you are done recording, click the Stop button (Figure 40). Click Play to review the recording. If you are satisfied with the recording, click OK to insert the audio icon and controls for the recording onto the slide. Or if you want to remake the recording, click Record again and start over.

5. Refer to steps 3 through 6 above to configure the audio clip.

TIP Sound effects are an animation option covered in Chapter 3, p. 41.

TIP Refer to Chapter 6 "Delivering a Presentation" to learn how to record narration for your entire slide show.

Table 15 Playback Tab

Play	Click to hear the audio.
Bookmarks group	Contains commands to mark or clear a position on the audio timeline. Click the Play button below the audio on the slide. When the desired sound is heard, click Add Bookmark. A mark is added to the audio timeline. During a presentation you need only click the bookmark to jump to that point in the audio. Bookmarks can also be used to trigger an animation (refer to TIP on p. 41). To remove a bookmark, click the marker and click Remove Bookmark.
Trim Audio	Click to display a dialog box where you can drag start and stop markers to trim the audio length.
Fade Duration	Commands to change the Fade In and Fade Out times for a fade effect at the beginning or end of audio.
Volume	Click to select a volume level for audio playback.
Audio Options group	You can manually click an option to select it. When Play in Background in the Audio Styles group is selected, several of these options are set automatically.
Audio Styles group	Click Play in Background for PowerPoint to set audio options to play the audio clip across the entire presentation. Click No Style if you want to manually set options.

Chapter 5
Objects, Charts, and Photo Album

A PowerPoint presentation can include content from other applications. A chart offers the audience a graphical interpretation of data. The Photo Album presentation is a favorite of business professionals and personal users alike.

Embedding and Linking Objects

The easiest way to incorporate content from multiple sources into your PowerPoint slides is by copying and pasting. For example, Word text or tables can be copied onto slides, and so can Excel cells and charts.

There are several options for pasting content from other sources. One option uses a process called object linking and embedding, or *OLE*. An *embedded* object is part of the PowerPoint presentation. A *linked* object will update in your presentation if the external file changes. In either case, OLE allows you to edit objects in their native application.

To insert Word text, a Word table, Excel cells, or an Excel Chart on the current slide:

1. Display the Word document and then select text or click the Table Move Handle to select a table.

    Or

    Display the Excel spreadsheet and then select cells or click a chart area to select a chart.

2. Click Home ⇨ Copy. For best results, leave the source file open until after pasting data.

3. Switch to PowerPoint and display the slide to receive the content.

4. Click in the content placeholder, if necessary. For example, if you are pasting content for a bulleted list, then click in a bullet item. If you do not click in a placeholder, the pasted content will be inserted as an object.

5. Click Home ⇨ Paste. The content is inserted and the Paste Options button appears.

6. Click Paste Options and point to the buttons (Figure 41) for a description and preview of their effect on the pasted content. The options allow you to change the format and theme of pasted content. Depending on the content, there may also be options to embed or link. Click an option, if desired.

Figure 41 Left to right: Use Destination Styles, Keep Source Formatting, Embed, Picture, Keep Text Only.

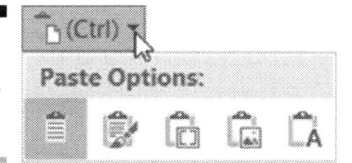

7. *Optional.* If content was pasted as an object, drag the handles on the content frame (Figure 42) to change its size, or drag the edge of the frame to move the object.

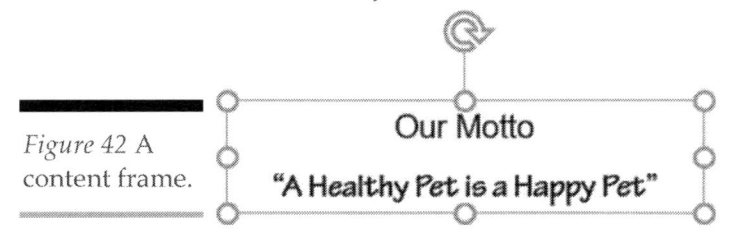

Figure 42 A content frame.

Our Motto
"A Healthy Pet is a Happy Pet"

8. *Optional.* If you chose to embed a Word table (using Paste Options), double-click the table to activate a Word application window for editing the content (Figure 43). Click outside the active frame to return to PowerPoint. Edits are embedded in PowerPoint and will not affect the original file.

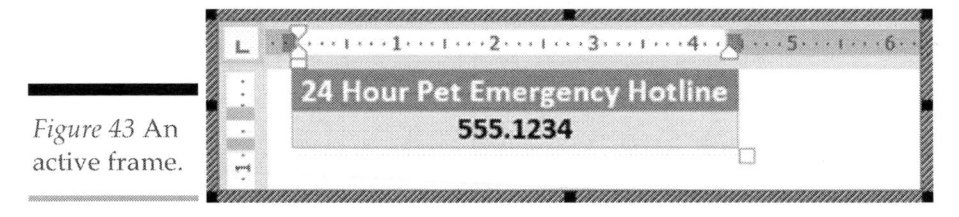

Figure 43 An active frame.

24 Hour Pet Emergency Hotline
555.1234

9. *Optional.* If you chose to embed Excel cells (using Paste Options), double-click the cells to activate an Excel application window for editing the content. You can also change the number of cells displayed by dragging a handle on the active content frame. Click outside the content frame to return to PowerPoint. Edits are embedded in PowerPoint and will not affect the original file.

Chapter 5 Objects, Charts, and Photo Album 69

10. *Optional*. Charts are linked by default. Click Chart Tools Design ⇨ Edit Data to open the spreadsheet to edit data, if needed. Close the spreadsheet window when done. Edits are saved to the source file and the PowerPoint chart.

11. *Optional*. If you chose to embed a chart (using Paste Options), click Chart Tools Design ⇨ Edit Data to activate an Excel application window for editing the content. Close the spreadsheet window when done. Edits are embedded in PowerPoint and will not affect the original file.

12. *Optional*. Refer to Table 16, p. 73 to edit a pasted chart.

You can also specify embedding or linking options before content is pasted. This is also the only way to link Word text and Excel cells.

To specify embed or link options:

1. Follow steps 1 through 3 above.
2. Click Home ⇨ Paste ⇨ Paste Special. A dialog box is displayed.
3. To embed the content, click Paste and then select the appropriate object type in the As list.

    Or

    To link the content, click Paste link and then select the appropriate object type in the As list. You can also optionally click Display as Icon to insert an icon that you click at presentation time to display the content source file.
4. Click OK. The content is pasted as an embedded or linked object.
5. *Optional*. Double-click the object and make edits. Click outside the frame or close the file when finished. Keep in mind that edits to embedded content appear only on the slide, while edits to linked content appear in the external file as well as the slide.

TIP Linked source files must remain in the same location on the computer with the presentation.

TIP If a linked chart was edited in the source file, click Chart Design ⇨ Refresh Data to update the chart on the slide.

TIP Click the Clipboard dialog box launcher on the Home tab to open a pane with copied items.

TIP To insert a new spreadsheet, Click Insert ⇨ Table ⇨ Excel Spreadsheet.

Linking to Screenshots

Another option for linking to a file is to format a screenshot as an action object. Click the screenshot action object during a presentation to open the linked document in its own window.

To add a linked screenshot to the current slide:

1. Open the document for linking and scroll to the area to use as a screenshot.
2. Click Insert ➪ Screenshot ➪ Screen Clipping. Drag to create a screenshot. The image is added to the slide.
3. Select the screenshot, if necessary, and click Insert ➪ Action to link the screenshot to the file (Chapter 4, p. 58).

Charts

Sometimes the easiest way to understand data relationships is through charts. Often, it's easier to create a chart in Excel, especially if you have a lot of data. But for a simple chart, you can create one directly in PowerPoint.

To add a new embedded chart to the current slide:

1. Click in the content placeholder where you want the chart to appear and then click Insert ➪ Chart. A dialog box is displayed (Figure 44). Chart types are listed in the left pane of the dialog box with an example of the selected chart to the right.

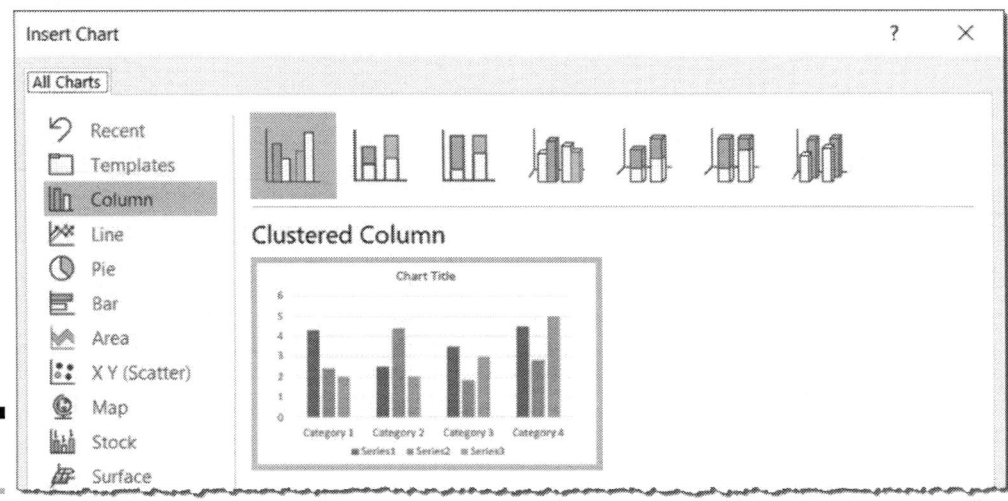

Figure 44

Chapter 5 Objects, Charts, and Photo Album 71

When picking a chart type, ask yourself what the purpose of the chart is. Will it compare data (bar chart)? Show a trend over time (line graph)? Or explain data as parts of a whole (pie chart)? Other special purpose chart types include Map for comparing data across geographic regions and Funnel for data that is progressively decreasing.

2. Click a chart type in the left pane of the dialog box for a preview. Click a variation above the chart example. Keep in mind that a chart is based on one or more *data series* (y values) and corresponding *category labels* (x values). For example, a pie chart has only one data series while a bar chart can compare numerous data series. If you will be entering more than one set of values for corresponding x values, then you cannot use a pie chart to represent the data.

3. Click OK. The chart is added as an object to the slide with a spreadsheet containing placeholder data, similar to Figure 45.

Figure 45 A new chart with placeholder data.

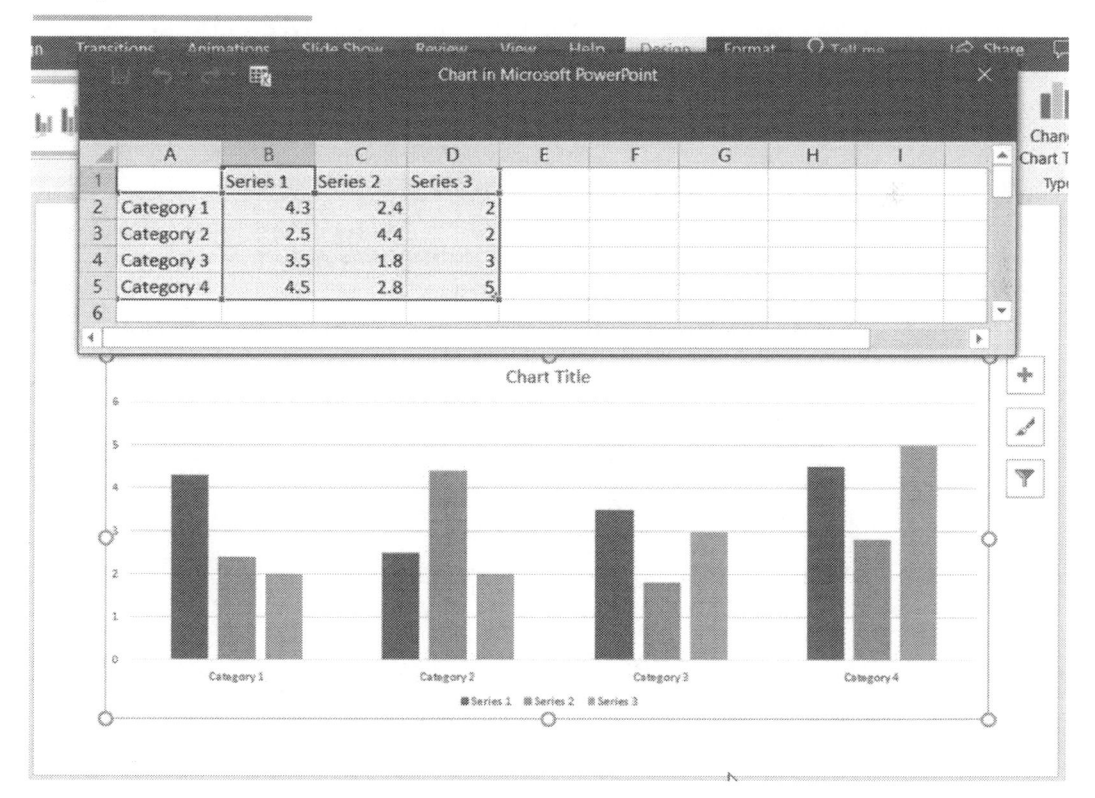

4. Click in each spreadsheet cell containing data and type your data. You will need to change the Category and Series labels as appropriate as well as data values. Delete any extra placeholder data by clicking the cell and pressing the Delete key. Use the scroll bars on the right and below the spreadsheet to bring hidden cells into view, if necessary.

5. After entering the data for your chart, click Close X in the upper-right of the spreadsheet. At any time, you can edit data values by right-clicking your chart and then selecting Edit Data.

6. *Optional*. Click the chart, if necessary, to make it active so that the chart tools buttons are available:

    Click Chart Elements and then click a checkbox to add or remove titles, legends, labels, and so on. Point to an option and click the arrow for placement commands and the More Options command, which displays a Format pane.

    Click Chart Styles to change the style and color of the chart.

    Click Chart Filters to change the data used for the chart.

7. *Optional*. Drag a corner handle on chart to **size** the object. To **move** the chart, drag the edge with the four-headed move pointer. Select a chart and then press the Delete key to **remove** it.

8. *Optional*. A chart is a collection of graphic objects. For example, you can click an individual pie slice and then drag it away from the other slices. To format text within an object, first double-click to place the insertion point.

9. *Optional*. Click a chart to select it and then use commands on the Chart Tools tab to choose layout and style options (Table 16, p. 73).

10. *Optional*. Click a chart to select it and then use commands on the Format tab to format individual objects (Table 16, p. 73).

TIP Refer to "Embedding and Linking Objects" in this chapter to learn about inserting an existing Excel chart.

TIP Refer to *Microsoft Excel 2016 In 90 Pages* to learn about chart types and more on formatting a chart.

Table 16 Chart Tabs

Chart Design Tab

Add Chart Element	Click for commands to add, remove, and change the placement of titles, labels, legends, and more. Click More Options in any submenu to display a Format pane.
Quick Layout	Click for a gallery of suggested layouts.
Change Colors	Click for available color schemes.
Chart Styles group	Click More ⏷ in the Chart Styles group for a gallery of styles. Point to a style to preview the effect. Click a style to apply it.
Switch Row/Column	Click to reverse the data over the axis.
Select Data	Click to display a dialog box for changing the data range for the chart.
Edit Data	Click to display the spreadsheet associated with the chart.
Refresh Data	Click to update a chart to reflect source data.
Change Chart Type	Click to display a dialog box for changing the chart type.

Format Tab

Chart Elements list [Chart Area ⏷]	Click the list arrow to display the elements of your chart. The series elements will vary. Click an element to make it active for formatting.
Format Selection	Click to open a Format pane with options for the selected element.
Reset to Match Style	Click to clear custom formatting for a selected element.
Insert Shapes group	Click a shape and then drag in the chart area to create a custom object.
Shape Styles group	Select an element and then use the Shape Styles group to customize formatting. Click More ⏷ in the Shape Styles group for a gallery of styles.

WordArt Styles group	Select an element and then use the WordArt Styles group to customize the look of text.
Alt Text	Click to open the Alt Text pane to type a description for screen readers.
Arrange group	Click Selection Pane to open a pane where objects on the chart can be selected. Use the arrange commands to position the selected object.
Size group	Used to change the dimensions of the chart. Click the Size task pane launcher for more options.

Photo Album Presentation

Do you want a presentation that simply displays slides of photos, one after another? Perhaps you have a new product line, customer testimonials, or photos from the company retreat. PowerPoint makes it easy to inform with a photo album slide show.

To create a photo album presentation:

1. Click Insert ⇨ Photo Album. (This command will create a new presentation even if editing an existing presentation.) The Photo Album dialog box is displayed (Figure 46).

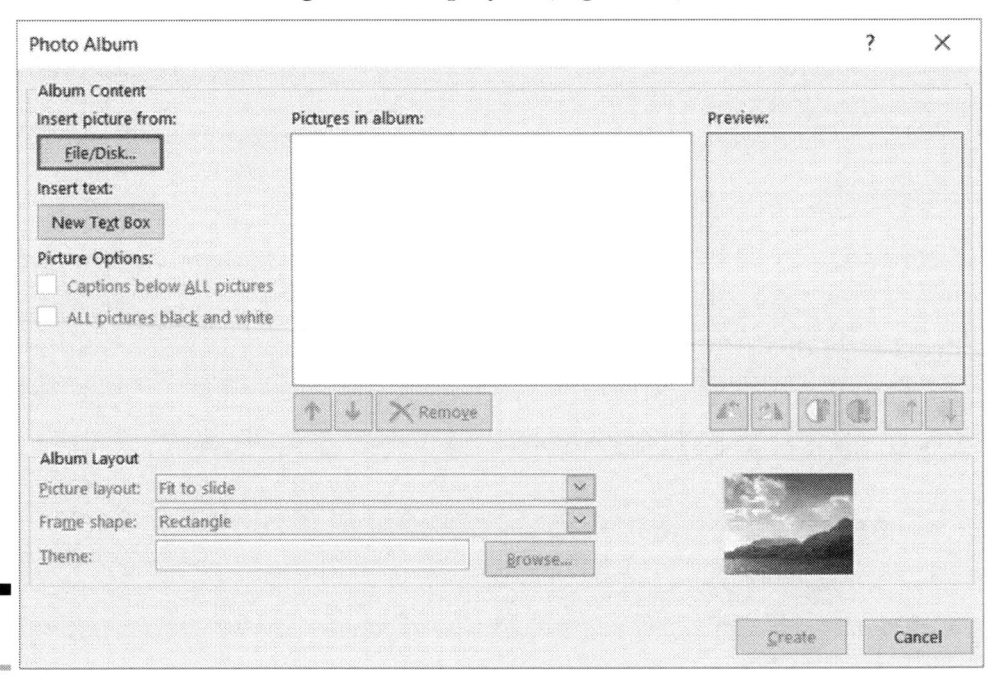

Figure 46

Chapter 5 Objects, Charts, and Photo Album 75

2. Click File/Disk and then navigate to the location of the photo to insert. To select multiple photos from the same folder, press and hold the Ctrl key while you click photos. Click Insert. (You may want to group all the photos for the slide show into the same folder before you begin).

   Or

   Click New Text Box to insert a text box, which can be edited after the photo album is created.

3. Continue to repeat Step 2 until all the photos and text boxes are added to the Photo Album dialog box. (You can always edit the presentation later to add more.)

4. *Optional*. In the Album Layout group:
   - Click Picture Layout and select an option.
   - Frame Shape is available if Picture Layout has been changed to a layout other than Fit to Slide. Click Frame Shape to select the way the photos are framed.
   - Click Browse to change the Theme. The theme can also be changed from the Design tab after the photo album is complete, which is often easier.

5. *Optional*. In the Pictures in album list, click a corresponding check box and then use the up and down arrow and Remove buttons below the list to change the order or delete items.

6. *Optional*. In the Pictures in album list, click a corresponding picture check box and then use the buttons below the Preview to edit the image (Figure 47).

Figure 47 Photo editing buttons. From left to right: Rotate Clockwise, Rotate Counter Clockwise, Increase Contrast, Decrease Contrast, Increase Brightness, Decrease Brightness.

7. *Optional*. In the Pictures Options:
   - Click Captions below ALL pictures, which is available when Picture layout is not Fit to slide. You can modify the captions after the photo album is created by double-clicking in the caption on each slide and typing new text.

- Click ALL pictures black and white for a monochrome presentation.

8. Click Create. A new presentation is created with the photos and textboxes you added. Edit the title slide, any textboxes you added, and if necessary, edit photo captions.

9. *Optional*. Use the Animations tab to apply an animation (p. 39) to a selected picture or textbox.

10. *Optional*. Use the Transitions tab to apply a slide transition (p. 36). Click Transitions ⇨ Apply to All to apply the same transition to every slide.

11. *Optional*. Each slide in a photo presentation is typically viewed for the same amount of time. To set up your presentation so that the slides automatically advance after a certain amount of time, click Transitions ⇨ Advance Slide ⇨ After and then change After to the desired display duration. Click Transitions ⇨ Apply to All to apply the same timing to every slide. When you click Slide Show ⇨ From Beginning the slides will advance based on your timings.

TIP Refer to Chapter 6 "Delivering a Presentation" to learn more about timings and how to play your photo album continuously.

Chapter 6
Delivering a Presentation

After carefully crafting your presentation, make the most of it by understanding how you can create custom slide shows, deliver to a live audience or one online, and record your presentation for distribution.

Delivering to a Live Audience

A successful presentation has a smooth delivery, which requires putting in the time to practice it. The steps required to rehearse a presentation are the same as the steps for delivering a presentation to a live audience. Refer also to Figure 52 and Table 18 on p. 83 for a complete list of options, including how to present online to an audience following along in a web browser.

To rehearse/deliver a presentation to a live audience:

1. Click Slide Show ⇨ From Beginning or click Slide Show ▼ in the status bar. The first slide is shown in Slide Show view.

    Or

    Click Slide Show ⇨ Custom Slide Show ⇨ Custom Shows for a dialog box. Click New to choose and order existing slides into a new custom show. Or click an existing custom show name.

2. Move the mouse pointer to the area in the lower-left of the slide to display the control bar (Figure 48).

    Figure 48 The control bar. Left to right: Previous, Next, Pen and Laser Pointer Tools, See All Slides, Zoom, and a menu.

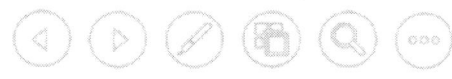

3. If you are rehearsing a presentation using just one monitor (your computer), then click the menu control ⋯ and select Show Presenter View to use Presenter View (Figure 49). If you are already connected to your output display, then Presenter View will display on your monitor if Slide Show ⇨ Use Presenter View was previously selected.

Microsoft PowerPoint 2019 in 90 pages **78**

*You can go directly to Presenter View from Normal view by pressing Alt+F5, allowing you to skip steps 1 through 3.

Figure 49 Presenter View.

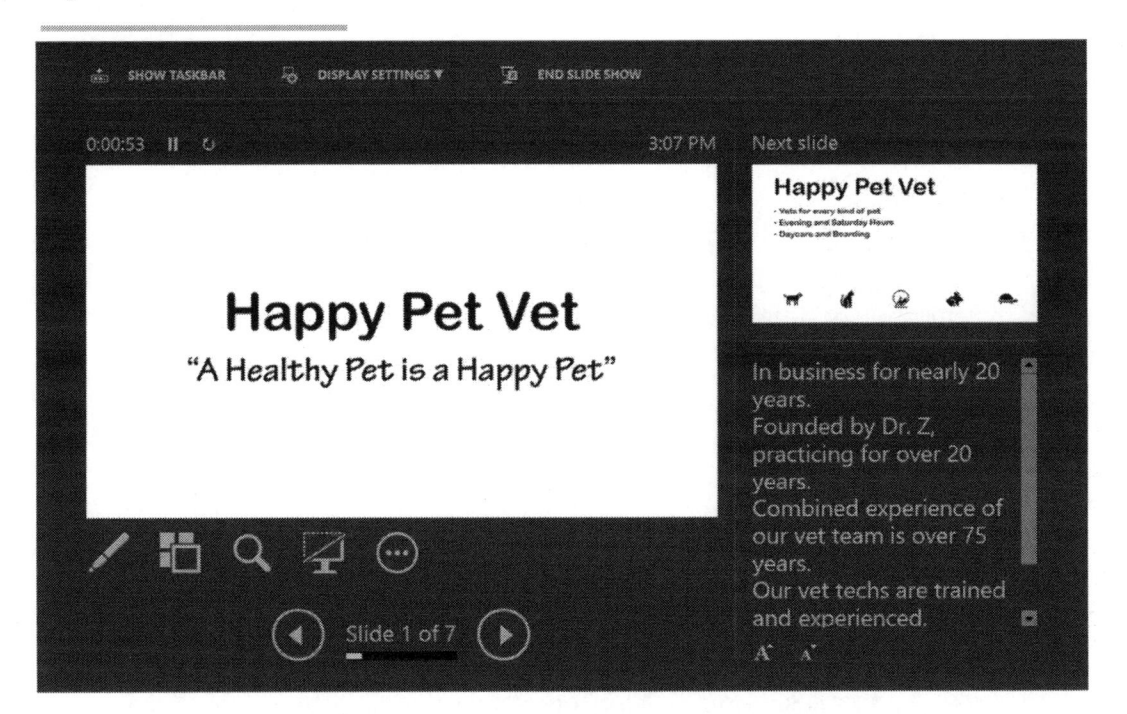

4. Use the Previous and Next controls on Slide Show view or Presenter View to navigate through the animations and slides. Or use keyboard shortcuts to navigate (Table 17, p. 79). (In the Tell Me box, type "keyboard shortcuts to deliver a presentation" for more keyboard shortcuts.)

5. *Optional.* Click the Pen and Laser Pointer Tools control in either Slide Show view or Presenter View and select a tool for inking, highlighting, or just pointing to areas of a slide. Press Esc to stop inking.

6. *Optional.* Click the See All Slides control in either Slide Show view or Presenter View and select a slide to jump to in the presentation. To return to the previous location, you will need to use See All Slides again.

7. *Optional.* Click the Zoom control in either Slide Show view or Presenter View and then click an area of the slide to magnify the content in the zoom box. Press Esc to return to the full slide.

8. *Optional.* You can temporarily blank the screen if you want to draw audience attention away from the slide (for example, to bring their focus to what you're saying). In Slide Show view, click (⋯) ⇨ Screen and then choose a command to change the screen display. In Presenter View, click the Black and unblack slide show control below the current slide.

9. Press the Esc key to end the presentation at any time.

TIP In Presenter View, a timer above the current slide keeps track of elapsed time. During rehearsals, the timer can be reset and paused, allowing you to practice until you get the timing to where you need it to be. To practice in full-screen and save your timings, click Slide Show ⇨ Rehearse Timings. Saved timings will be used for a show when Slide Show ⇨ Use Timings is selected.

TIP To switch the display with Presenter View, click Display Settings at the top of Presenter View and then click Swap Presenter View and Slide Show.

TIP A Bluetooth digital pen paired to your computer can also be used to navigate a presentation. Press the eraser once to advance; press and hold the eraser to reverse.

Table 17 Slide Show Keyboard Shortcuts

Start a Presentation	F5 to start at beginning of presentation Shift+F5 to start at the current slide Alt+F5 to start in Presenter View
Perform the next animation or advance to the next slide	N, Enter, Page Down, Right Arrow, Down Arrow, or Spacebar
Perform the previous animation or return to the previous slide	P, Page Up, Up Arrow, Left Arrow, or Backspace
Go to a slide	Type the slide number and then press Enter.
View all slides	Ctrl+S
Toggle between a blank slide	B or period for a black slide W or comma for a white slide
End a presentation	Esc

Use Timings to Deliver a Presentation

Some slide shows, such as one that will run at a kiosk, are suitable for preset timings for advancing the slides. A presentation that uses timings can also be set up as self-running show that loops continuously or exported as a video that can be emailed or uploaded to a website.

To record timings:

1. Click Slide Show ⇨ Rehearse Timings. The slide show is started, and the Rehearsal toolbar is displayed in the upper left of the first slide. Presenter View is not an option when recording timings.
2. Click the Rehearsal toolbar Next button → or click the mouse or use keyboard shortcuts (Table 17, p. 79) to navigate through the animations and slides at a rate you want your audience to experience.
3. *Optional.* If you want to redo the timings for a slide, click the Repeat button ↺ on the timer. You can also pause recording with the Pause button ∥ on the timer. (Click Pause again to restart.)
4. Press Esc to end the presentation. You will be prompted to save or discard the timings. Note that timings can always be redone, and previous timings discarded.
5. *Optional.* Click View ⇨ Slide Sorter. Note that slides display their timings. You can reorder slides or create a custom slide show (see Step 1 in "Delivering to a Live Audience") without having to record timings again because timings stay with a slide until cleared.
6. *Optional.* Click Slide Show ⇨ Record Slide Show ⇨ Clear for options to clear timings.

To set up a self-running presentation:

1. Click Slide Show ⇨ Set Up Slide Show. A dialog box is displayed (Figure 50).

Chapter 6 Delivering a Presentation 81

Figure 50 Set Up Show dialog box.

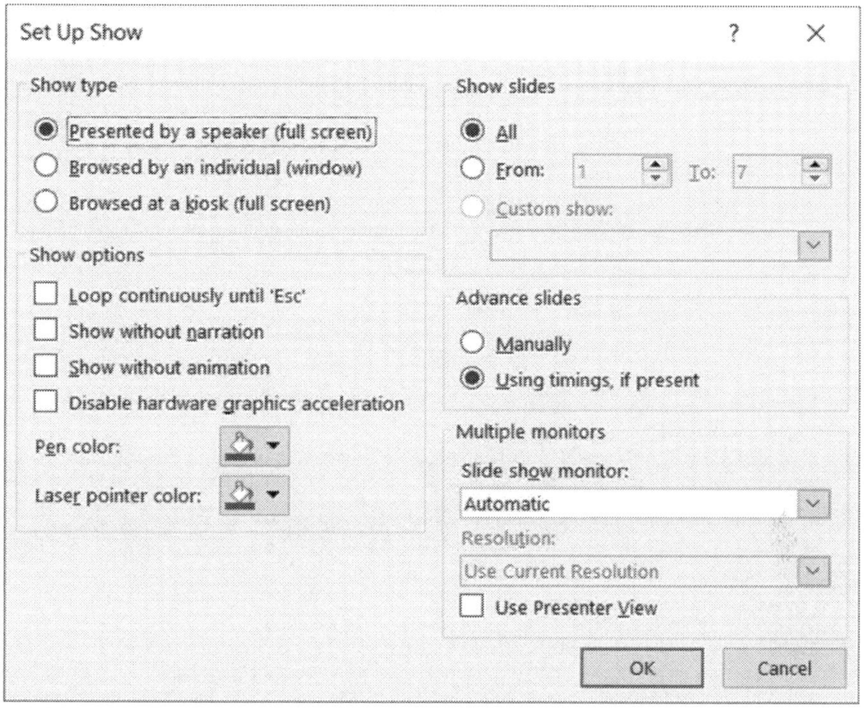

2. To create a slide show that is displayed continuously at a kiosk or other similar setup, be sure Use timings, if present is selected and then click Browsed at a kiosk (full screen). The Loop continuously until 'Esc' option will be automatically selected.

3. Click OK. The next time you click Slide Show ⇨ From Beginning the show will start and run continuously until you press Esc.

4. *Optional.* If you want to distribute the slide show as a video (.mp4 or .wmv), click File ⇨ Export and then click Create a Video. Select a quality from the top drop-down list and then select Use Recorded Timings and Narrations from the second drop-down list and click Create Video.

TIP You do not need to record separate timings for a Photo Album slide show if you previously set the Advance Slide option on the Transitions tab with timings for each slide. Refer to p. 76. With these timings, you can export the slide show as a video (Step 4 above) that can be emailed or posted.

Deliver a Presentation as a Recording

When you want to include narration, laser pointer movements, and ink in a self-running or video presentation, you need to record the slide show.

To record a presentation:

1. Verify that you have a sound card, microphone, speakers, and optionally, a webcam.
2. Click Slide Show ⇨ Record Slide Show ⇨ Record from Beginning. The Record Slide Show View is displayed (Figure 51).

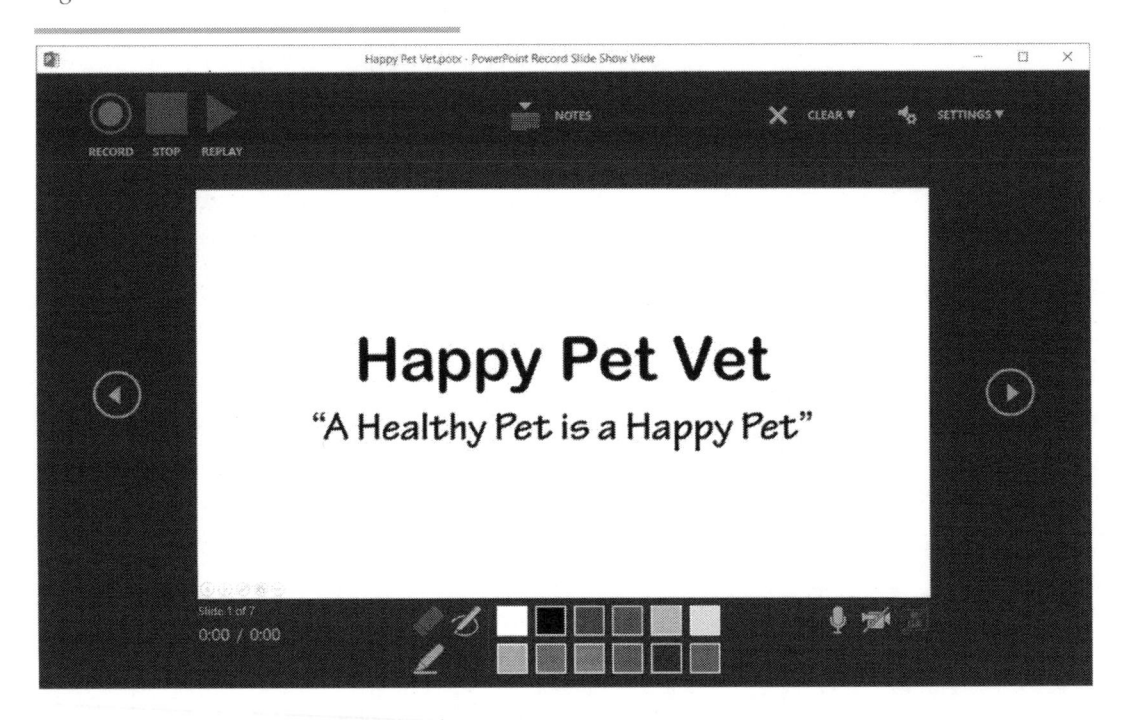

Figure 51 Record Slide Show View.

3. Click SETTINGS at the top of Record Slide Show View to choose microphone and video equipment.
4. Click RECORD to start the recording. A three-second countdown begins the recording.
5. *Optional.* Click NOTES to display your speaker notes for a slide.
6. *Optional.* Click a pen, ink, or highlighter and select a color. Annotations on the slide will be recorded. Press Esc to return to the arrow pointer.

Chapter 6 Delivering a Presentation

7. Click the Next and Previous controls on the right and left of the slide to navigate through the animations and slides. Or click the mouse or use keyboard shortcuts to navigate (Table 17, p. 79).

   *Do not narrate during a slide transition and pause briefly at the beginning and end of each slide to avoid hearing gaps in narration.

8. Click STOP or press the S key to stop the recording. Press Esc to return to Normal view.

9. *Optional.* Click View ⇨ Slide Sorter. Note that slides display their timings. You can reorder slides or create a custom slide show (see Step 1 in "Delivering to a Live Audience") without having to re-record because timings and narration stay with a slide until cleared.

10. *Optional.* Click Slide Show ⇨ Record Slide Show ⇨ Clear for options to clear timings.

11. *Optional.* You can start a recording at the current slide and end the recording immediately after to replace the narration and timing for just one slide.

12. *Optional.* If you want to distribute the recording as a video (.mp4 or .wmv), click File ⇨ Export and then click Create a Video. Select a quality from the top drop-down list and then select Use Recorded Timings and Narrations from the second drop-down list and click Create Video.

TIP Click File ⇨ Options and then click Customize Ribbon. In the Main Tabs list, click Recording and then click OK. A Recording tab is added to the Ribbon.

TIP You can record during a live audience presentation if you want to capture audience feedback and comments.

TIP File ⇨ Export commands can also be used to create a PDF of your presentation or package your presentation for CD. File ⇨ Share commands are used to email the presentation, present online, and publish slides to a library.

Figure 52 The Slide Show tab.

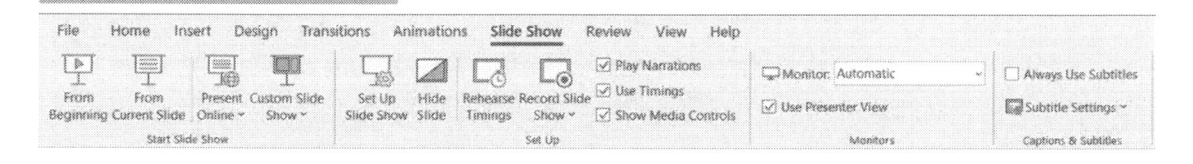

Table 18 Slide Show Tab

From Beginning	Click to display Slide Show view with the first slide in the presentation.
From Current Slide	Click to display Slide Show view with the current slide in the presentation.
Present Online	Click to set up your presentation to allow others to watch from a web browser.
Custom Slide Show	Click for a dialog box where you can choose and order slides from the current presentation to make a named custom presentation.
Set Up Slide Show	Click for a dialog box where you can select the show type, show options, slides to display, and more before you start a slide show. For example, if you do not want animations to play during your show, then clear that option. If you want to manually advance slides, then select Manually.
Hide Slide	Click to hide the current slide from the show.
Rehearse Timings	Click to start a slide show from the beginning while timing the show.
Record Slide Show	Click to record the slide show which can include narration, ink, and video. Recorded shows can be distributed or uploaded to YouTube.
Set Up group options	Select Play Narrations when you want recorded narrations and laser pointing to play back during a slide show. Select Use Timings when you want to use prerecorded timings to navigate through your show. Clear Show Media Controls when you have media set to start automatically.
Monitors group	Use the Monitors list to select the presentation output. Automatic is usually the best option to start with. Select Use Presenter View to allow full-screen slides on one display and speaker notes on your display.
Captions & Subtitles group	Use these options to set up captioning and subtitles for an accessible slide show.

Chapter 7
Special Purpose PowerPoint Features

A presentation often contains data from many different sources, which may require collaborating with others. Comments become imperative for communicating with collaborators or for just making a note to yourself. Understanding how you can make your slide show more accessible is important for getting your message across. For further in-depth coverage of a feature, type the topic in the Tell Me box and then select the related Get Help on command.

Using Multiple Windows

The View tab Window group has options that are helpful when developing a presentation (Table 19).

Table 19 View Tab Window Group

New Window	Opens another window with the same presentation so that you can view and work on different slides at the same time.
Arrange All	Stacks the opens windows.
Cascade	Organizes open presentations into overlapping windows.
Move Split	Click and then use the arrow keys to change the splits for panes.
Switch Windows	Click to display open presentations. Click a presentation name to switch to that window.

The Draw Tab

You can add your own freehand drawings, text highlighting, and ink strokes to a slide.

To customize the current slide:

1. Click Draw ⇨ Draw (or Draw with Touch) and then click a drawing tool in the Pens group. Refer to the Draw tab below. NOTE: If the Draw tab is not available on your Ribbon, click File ⇨ Options and then click Customize Ribbon. Select the Draw tab and click OK.
2. *Optional*. In the Pens group, click the Add Pen and select a new tool, thickness, and color.
3. Use the mouse or other device to draw on the slide.

    Press the Esc key when you want to revert back to the arrow pointer. The inked annotation is an object. Pointing to it changes the mouse pointer to the four-headed arrow pointer.
4. *Optional*. To erase ink, click Draw ⇨ Eraser and then click the inked area to remove. Click Eraser again or press the Esc key to stop erasing.
5. *Optional*. Click an inked object (with the four-headed arrow pointer) to select it and then use commands in the Shape Format tab, Table 13, p. 53, to change the color or thickness.

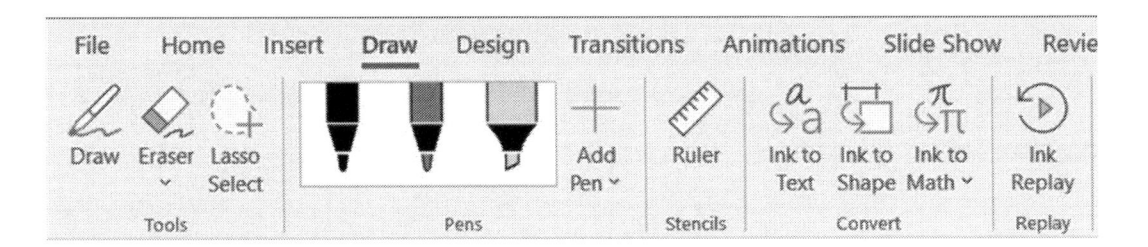

Table 20 Draw Tab

Tools group	Draw and Eraser are toggles (click the Eraser arrow for eraser types). Click once to activate the command. Click a second time or press the Esc key to deactivate. Click Lasso Select and then drag the crosshairs mouse pointer to encircle or "lasso" inked areas for multiple selection.

Chapter 7 Special Purpose PowerPoint Features   87

Pens group	Click a predefined style or click New Pen to add a new style.
Ruler	Click to add a straightedge for drawing. Use your fingers or the mouse scroll wheel to change the angle. Type Change ruler angle in the Tell Me box for more ways to adjust the ruler. Click Ruler a second time to remove it from the slide.
Ink to Text	Click and then select the ink to convert to text.
Ink to Shape	Click and then select the ink to a standard shape.
Ink to Math	Click and then select the ink to convert to standard mathematical symbols. Click Draw ⇨ Ink to Math ⇨ Open Ink Equation Editor for an editor where your drawing is converted to standard text and symbols.
Ink Replay	Click to replay ink strokes. Office 365 only.

Protecting a Presentation

There are several levels of protection that can be added to a presentation.

To protect a presentation:

1. Click File ⇨ Info and then click Protect Presentation. Several options are displayed.
1. If you want to make the file read only, click Always Open Read-Only, requiring the user to elect to make changes.
2. If you want to require a password to open the file in the future, click Encrypt with Password. A dialog box is displayed. Type a password, if desired. WARNING: A password cannot be retrieved if forgotten. Click OK. Retype the password and click OK again.
3. If you have a digital ID, click Add a Digital Signature to ensure the integrity of the presentation.
4. If you want to let users know the presentation is final, click Mark as Final. A dialog box notifies you that the presentation will be marked as final and saved.

Comments

Comments on a slide communicate with collaborators or provide a note to yourself. There can be multiple comments per slide, each indicated by a red comment bubble. The bubbles do not appear during a presentation.

To insert and manage comments:

1. Select a slide and then click in the area where you want the comment bubble to appear (you may also click an object).
2. Click Review ⇨ New Comment. A comment bubble is added to the slide and the Comments pane is opened.
3. Type the text for your comment and then click the slide or press Enter to complete the comment.
4. Use commands in the Comments group on the Review tab to edit, delete, and view comments.

TIP Right-click a comment bubble for Copy Text, New Comment, and Delete Comment commands.

TIP The Comment command is also on the Insert tab.

Collaboration

Collaboration on a presentation can take several forms. Since a presentation often contains content from other sources, such as an Excel spreadsheet or a Word document, collaborators can develop external documents that you later embed or link to the presentation (refer to Chapter 5).

[Share]

If you want collaborators to contribute to the development of the PowerPoint slides, you can share the presentation:

- Click Share in the upper-right of the PowerPoint window, upload the file to OneDrive, and then invite people through email to access the file.
- Collaborators can click the comment bubble next to the Share button to display the Comments pane where they can respond to comments that have been added to slides.

For more information, use the Tell Me box to get help on "share a presentation".

TIP Changes are automatically periodically saved to presentations stored in the cloud. Others can see updates in seconds.

TIP Click File ⇨ Options ⇨ Save and then click Embed fonts in the file before sharing.

TIP Another form of collaboration uses the Review ⇨ Compare command to compare and combine two presentations.

Creating a Template

A custom template saves time when you need to create presentations with a similar theme over and over again.

Before creating your first template:

1. Click File ⇨ Options and then click Save.
2. Type a location for your templates in the Default personal templates location and click OK. (You may need to create the folder first, if the one you want does not already exist.)

To create a template from a new presentation:

1. Create a new Blank presentation.
2. Refer to Chapter 3 to add and modify the theme, formats, graphics, and other unchanging data for your template.
3. Click File ⇨ Export.
4. Click Change File Type and then click Template (*.potx).
5. Click Save As below the file type list. A dialog box is displayed with PowerPoint Template as the file type.
6. Browse to the location to store the template (if necessary), type a File Name, and click Save.

To use a template file for a new presentation:

1. Click File ⇨ New.
2. Above the featured templates, click Personal. Your personal template files are displayed.
3. Click a template. A new presentation is created based on your template.

TIP You can also save an existing presentation as a template clicking File ⇨ Save As and then selecting PowerPoint Template (*.potx) as the file type.

Making a Presentation Accessible

Consider accessibility as you create your slides for a better overall presentation. One tip is to use strong contrast between text and backgrounds and make sure fonts are sans serif, at least 18 points, with plenty of white space around.

To determine other ways to make your presentation more accessible, click Review ⇨ Check Accessibility. An Accessibility pane is displayed with a list of issues to be examined.

Document Inspector

The final check for a document that will be shared electronically is to remove personal information and hidden data. As helpful as it may be to wipe your document of this type data, which is referred to as *metadata*, you will also want to perform the check on a copy of your document because the metadata may not be able to be restored. The document inspector can also be used to alert you to accessibility and compatibility issues.

To remove personal information and hidden data:

1. Save your presentation.
1. Click File ⇨ Save As and save your presentation using a new name. (p. 9.)
2. Click File ⇨ Info and then click Check for Issues ⇨ Inspect Document. A dialog box is displayed.
3. Read through the options and clear any content you do not want reviewed.
4. Click Inspect. A report is displayed.
5. Review the results and click Remove All where you want metadata to be deleted.
6. Click Close to remove the dialog box.

Index

.com, 57
@, 57
¢, 17
©, 16
®, 16
¼, 16
½, 16
365, ix
3D model, 55
á, 17
™, 16

A

accessibility, ix, 4, 90
accessibility, checking, 90
Account command, 10
Action Buttons, 55
Action Buttons group, shapes, 59
Action command, 58, 70
action object, screenshot, 70
action objects, 55, 58
active frame, object, 68
Add Animation command, 40
Add Bookmark command, 61, 66
Add Shape command, SmartArt, 57
adding text, 18
Advance Slide command, 76, 81
Alt key, ix
Alt text, 50, 61
Animation Pane, 41, 65
animation, bookmark trigger, 61, 66
animation, sound effects, 65
animations, 39
Animations tab, 3
application interface, 1

Arrange All command, 85
arrow keys, 6
arrow pointer, 8
arrow pointer, four-headed, 8, 18, 43, 44
arrow pointer, two-headed, 8
arrows, 54
audio, 64
audio clip, creating, 65
Audio command, 64
audio icon, 64
Audio on My PC command, 64
Audio Tools Format tab, *see* Playback tab
audio, play in background, 66
audio, recording, 65
AutoCorrect, 15, 16
AutoCorrect options, 10
AutoCorrect Options command, 16, 17
AutoFit, 15
AutoFit button, 17
AutoFormat, 15

B

background audio, controlling, 65
Background Removal tab, 49
Backspace key, 7, 20
Backstage view, 3, 9
banners, 54
bar chart, 71
Blank presentation, 1, 12
blank screen, during a presentation, 79
Bluetooth digital pen, 79

bookmark, as a trigger, 41, 61, 66
bookmark, audio, 66
bookmark, video, 61
branding, 31
Browse button, 9
bullet style, changing, 15
bullet level, changing, 15
bulleted list, SmartArt, 56
bullets in a placeholder, 15
button shapes, action object, 58

C

call to action, 11
captions, in photo album, 75
category labels, in a chart, 71
Cell Margins command, 45
cell, changing size, 45
cell, table, 41
Change Shape command, SmartArt, 57
Chart command, 70
Chart Design tab, 73
Chart Elements button, 72
Chart Filters button, 72
Chart Styles button, 72
Chart Tools Design tab, *see* Chart Design tab
Chart Tools Format tab, *see* Format tab
chart, creating, 71
chart, editing, 72
chart, linking or embedding, 69
Clear command, 80, 83
Clear WordArt command, 23
clearing a selection, 18
click, 8
Clipboard, 19, 69
Clipboard group, 26
close a document, 3
Close command, 9

Close Master View command, 34
Close X, 5, 10
cloud, 89
Collaboration, 3
collaboration on a presentation, 45, 88
Color/Grayscale group, 30
comments, adding to a slide, 3, 87
comments, collaboration, 3, 88
Compare command, 89
content frame, embedding and linking, 68
content placeholder, 4
Control (Ctrl) key, 6
control bar, in a slide show, 77
Control Dock, screen recording, 62
Convert to SmartArt command, 57
converting, file type, 9
Copy command, 19
Copy command, embedding and linking, 67
Copy Link command, 58
Copy Text command, 88
copyright, pictures, 47
Creative Commons licenses, 47
Crop to Shape command, 50
crosshair pointer, 54
Ctrl key, 6
Ctrl+C, 19
Ctrl+S, 6, 10
Ctrl+V, 19
Ctrl+X, 19
Ctrl+Z, 16, 58
Custom Slide Show command, 77
Custom Slide Size command, 12
Customize Ribbon command, 83
customizing PowerPoint, 10
Cut command, 18, 19

D

data series, in a chart, 71

Index

Date & Time command, 28
Delete Comment command, 88
Delete key, 7, 18, 20
Delete Slide command, 14
deleting text, 18
Design Ideas button, 32
Design tab, 3, 31
Desktop, 1
dialog box launcher, 3
digital ID, 87
digital pen, 79
distribute a presentation, 3
document, final check, 90
document inspector, 90
Document Inspector, 9
document, linking to, 58
dotted border, 8
double-click, 8
drag, 8
Draw Borders group, 44
Draw tab, 18, 86
Draw Table command, 43
Drawing group, 24
Drawing Tools Format tab, *see* Shape Format tab
Duplicate Selected Slides command, 14, 38
Duplicate Slide command, 14

E

Edit Alt Text command, 64
Edit Data command, 69
Editing a presentation, 18
Effect Options command, 36, 40
Email command, 9
email, linking to, 58
emailing a document, 9
embed code, video, 60
embedding objects, 67, 68
End key, 7

Enter key, 6
Equation tab, 17
Equation Tools Design tab, *see* Equation tab
equation, inserting, 17, 18, 87
Eraser command, 45, 86
Escape (Esc) key, 6
Excel cells, embedding or linking, 67
Excel charts, embed or link, 67
Excel Spreadsheet command, 43, 69
Export command, 9, 81, 83, 89

F

fade effect, audio, 66
fade effect, video, 62
File name, 3
File tab, 3, 9
file, linking to presentation, 70
Find command, 20
floating objects, 48
flow chart, SmartArt, 56
Font and Paragraph group, 22
Font dialog box, 22
fonts, replacing, 21
footer, adding, 28
Format Background command, 32, 35, 49
Format Background task pane, 32, 49
Format Painter command, 26
    double-clicking, 27
Format Shape task pane, 23, 25, 53
Format tab, 73
Format Video pane, 61
formats, copying, 26
formatting text, 21
freehand drawings, inserting, 86
Freeze Panes command, 85
From Beginning command, 30, 77, 81
From Current Slide command, 30
Funnel chart, 71

G

GIF, 47
graphics, *see* Pictures
graphics, hide, 35
grayscale or black and white, viewing, 30
gridlines, displaying, 44, 51
guides, displaying, 51

H

hand shape pointer, 8
handle, object, 8
handles, placeholder, 14
Handouts Master command, 34
Header & Footer command, 28
header, adding, 28
help, 4
Hide command, 85
highlighting text, 18, 86
highlighting, during presentation, 78
Home key, 7
Home tab, 3
    editing commands, 19
hourglass pointer, 7
hyperlink, 8, 57
hyperlink, inserting, 57

I

I-beam pointer, 8
Icon command, 55
icon, using as link to source file, 69
iframe embed code, 60
image, corrections, 50
image, reduce file size, 50
image, see also photo, 50
image, sharpen, 50
Info command, 9, 90
Ink Equation command, 18
ink in a self-running or video presentation, 82
ink strokes, inserting, 86
Ink to Math command, 86
Ink to Shape command, 86
inking, during a presentation, 78
input devices, 6
Insert Layout command, 34
Insert Link command, 57
Insert New Equation command, 17
Insert tab, 3
Insert Table command, 42
insertion point, 6
Intelligent Services, 32

J

JPEG, 47

K

keyboard, 6
    symbols and special characters, 17
keyboard shortcuts, ix
kiosk, delivering a presentation, 80

L

laser pointer movements, 82
Layout command, 14
layout, reapply, 34
Layout tab, 43, 45
lightbulb, 4
line graph, 71
lines shape, 54
link, inserting a hyperlink, 57
linked object, 67
linking objects, 69
live audience presentation, recording, 83
loop continuously, 80

M

magnification of slide, 4
Map chart, 71
mathematical equation, 17, 86
Maximize button, 3
Media group, 64, 65
Merge Cells command, 45
metadata, 90
microphone, 65, 82
Microsoft Office 2019, 1
mini toolbar, 22
Minimize button, 3
monitors, for presentation output, 84
Morph command, 39
Morph transition, 37, 41, 55
motion path animation, 39
mouse, 6, 7
move pointer, 49
moving text, 18
mp4, 59, 81, 83
multiple selection, inked areas, 86
music, adding audio, 64

N

narration, adding audio, 64
narration, recording for slide show, 65, 82
New command, 9, 89
New Comment command, 88
New screen, 12
New Slide command, 13
New Window command, 85
Next button, Rehearsal toolbar, 80
Next control, 78
Next control, Record Slide Show View, 83
No Fill command, 44
Normal View, 4, 29
Notes button, 4

Notes Master command, 34
Notes Page command, 27
Notes pane, 4, 27

O

object
  action, 58
  embedded, 67
  linked, 67
  selecting, 20, 51
objects
  aligning, 51
  floating, 48
  grouping, 51
  moving, 51
  triggering display, 39
Office 365, ix
OLE, 67
On Bookmark command, 41
On Click of command, 40
OneDrive, 88
Online Pictures command, 47
Online Video command, 59
open a document, 3
Open command, 9
Open Link command, 58
Options command, 10, 83, 88, 89
organizational charts, 56
Outline View, 29
overhead projector, 12

P

Page Down (PgDn) key, 7
Page Up (PgUp) key, 7
pane, 5
password protect a presentation, 87
Paste command, 18, 19
Paste command, embedding and linking, 68

Paste Options button, 19, 68, 69
Paste Options command, 19
Paste Special command, 69
pasting text from Clipboard, 20
PDF attachment, 9
pen, Draw tab, 86
Pen and Laser Pointer Tools control, 78
personal information, removing, 90
Photo Album command, 74
photo album presentation, 64
photo album slide show, 74
Photo Album slide show, timings, 81
photo icon, SmartArt, 56
photo, cropping, 50
photo, see also *image*
photo, size, 50
photo, transparency, 50
Picture Format tab, 49, 51
Picture Tools Format tab, *see* Picture Format tab
picture, animating, 48
picture, as table background, 44
picture, linking to file, 48
picture, maintaining aspect ratio, 49
Pictures command, 47
pie chart, 71
placeholder
  active, 6
  content, 3
  formatting, 24
  inserting, 33
  selecting, 18
planning a presentation, 11
Play button, video, 60
Play in Background command, 64
Playback tab, 61, 66
point, 7, 8
pointer, 7
pointing, during a presentation, 78
Poster Frame command, 61

.potx, 89
PowerPoint, starting, 1
PowerPoint 2019 icon, 1
PowerPoint 2019 Quick Reference, ix, 5, 101
PowerPoint window, 1
presentation
  creating, 12
  design, 31
  design considerations, 11, 14
  mark as final, 87
  nonlinear navigation, 46
  previewing, 29
  protecting, 87
  rehearsing, 77
Presenter View, 77
Preserve command, 35
Previous control, 78
Previous control, Record Slide Show View, 83
print a document, 3
Print command, 9
Print Preview, 3
Proofing command, 17
protecting a presentation, *87*

Q

Quick Access toolbar, 3
  Undo and Redo, 19
Quick Access toolbar options, 10
Quick Access Toolbar, customize, 3
Quick Reference, ix, 5, 101
Quick Styles command, 24
quitting PowerPoint, 10

R

Reading View, 4, 29
Reading View Keyboard Shortcuts, 30
Recent, Start screen link, 1

Index

Record Audio command, 65
Record from Beginning command, 82
Record Slide Show View, 82
Recording tab, 83
recording timings, 80
Redo command, 3, 19
Refresh Data command, 69
Rehearsal toolbar, 80
Rehearse Timings command, 80
rehearsing a presentation, 77
Remove Background command, 49
Remove Bookmark command, 61, 66
Remove Link command, 58
Rename command, 33
Replace command, 21
Replace Fonts command, 21
Reset command, 14, 26
Reset Picture command, 50
Reuse Slides command, 14
Review tab, 3
Ribbon, 3
   shortcuts, ix
Ribbon command, finding, 5
Ribbon Display Options button, 3
Ribbon, hide, 3
right-click, 8
rotation handle, 49
rulers, displaying, 51
Ruler, Draw tab, 86

S

sans serif typeface, 21
Save As command, 9, 89, 90
Save button, 3, 10
saving a presentation, 10
Scalable Vector Graphic, 55
Screen Clipping command, 48, 70
Screen command, 79
Screen Recording command, 62
screen recording video, 60, 62

Screenshot command, 48, 70
screenshot, as link, 70
ScreenTips, ix, 7, 26
scroll wheel, 8, 87
search, 4
Section command, 45
Section Zoom command, 46
See All Slides control, *78*
Select All command, 20, 32
selecting a block, 20
selecting a placeholder, 18
selecting objects, 20, 51
selecting text, 18, 25
Selection Pane command, 20, 51
self-running show, 80
serif typeface, 21
Set Up Slide Show command, 80
Shape Fill command, 52
Shape Format tab, 22, 25, 34, 51, 52, 53, 55, 86
shape, customized, 53
Shapes command, 54, 59
Share command, 3, 9, 83, 88
Show Presenter View command, 77
slide
   adding, 13
   deleting, 14
   displaying in Reading View, 30
   how many to use, 11
   linking to, 46, 58
   reorder, 3, 29, 46, 83
   revealing, 36
   selecting, 32
Slide Master command, 33
Slide Master view, 23
Slide Number command, 28
Slide pane, 3
Slide pane, sizing, 4
slide show keyboard shortcuts, 79
Slide Show tab, 3, 84
Slide Show view, 4, 77

Slide Size command, 12
slide size, changing, 35
Slide Sorter view, 4, 29, 80, 83
Slide Zoom command, 58
Slides from Outline command, 14
smart guides, 49
Smart Lookup, 5
SmartArt command, 56
SmartArt Design tab, 56
SmartArt graphics, 56
SmartArt Tools Design tab, see SmartArt Design tab
sound card, 65, 82
sound effects, animations, 41
sound effects, transitions, 37
sound recordings, see also audio, 64
sound, action object, 59
source files, OLE, 69
speaker notes, 27
speakers, 65, 82
spelling checker, 15
spelling error, 16
Split command, 85
squiggly line, 16
Standard 4:3, 12
Start Inking command, 86
Start menu, 1
Start screen, 1, 9, 12
story, telling with PowerPoint, 11
Summary Zoom command, 46
SVG, 55
Swap Presenter View and Slide Show command, 79
symbols, inserting, 16, 17
Symbol command, 17

T

Tab key, 6
editing features, 19
Table Background command, 44
Table command, 42, 76, 79
Table Move Handle, 67
Table Style Options group, 43
Table Design tab, 43
Table Tools Design tab, see Table Design tab
Table Tools Layout tab, see Layout tab
tables for data display, 41
status bar options, 4
Taskbar, 1
Tell Me box, 4
template, 12
   creating, 89
   opening, 89
Text Box command, 52
text box, in a photo album, 75
text box, transparency, 53
text boxes, 52
Text Highlighter, 22
Text Pane command, 56
text, adding to a slide, 15
text, selecting, 18, 25
theme, 12, 31
theme, applying to selected slides, 32
Themes command, 33
thumbnails, 3, 4
TIF, 47
Timing group, animations, 40
Timing group, transitions, 37
timings, 37, 40, 80
timings, clearing, 80
timings, for advancing slides, 80
timings, in photo album, 76
Title Slide, 12, 13
toolbar, 3, 19, 22
Transitions tab, 3
transitions, 36
   good design, 37
   in photo album, 76
   narration, 83
   removing, 37

transparency, shapes, 55
transparency, text box, 52
transparency, pictures, 50

U

underline style
   avoiding confusion, 23
Undo, 3
Undo command, 19, 58
URL, creating a link, 58
Use Presenter View command, 77

V

Variants group, 31
Venn diagram, SmartArt, 56
video
   converting a presentation, 60
   export a presentation, 80
   export to Ultra HD (4K), 9
   inserting into a slide, 59
   playing, 59
   playing repeatedly, 62
   screen recording, 62
   trim length, 62
Video command, 59
Video Corrections Options command, 60
Video tabs, 60
Video Fomat tab, 60
Video Tools Format tab, *see* Video Format tab
Video Tools Playback tab, *see* Playback tab
View tab, 3, 85
View options, 4
Vimeo, 59

W

web page, linking to, 58
webcam, *82*
WebVTT file, *62*
Widescreen 16:9, 12
Window controls, 3
Windows 10, ix
wmv, 81, 83
Word outline, converting to a presentation, 14
Word table, copying, 43
Word tables, embedding or linking, 67
Word text, embedding or linking, 67
WordArt, 22
WordArt command, 53
WordArt in a table, 44
WordArt, chart, *73*
WordArt, shapes, 55
WordArt text box, 53
www., 57

X

X button, 3
x values, chart, 71

Y

y values, chart, 71
YouTube video, inserting, 60

Z

Zoom command, 46, 58
Zoom control, 79
Zoom controls, 4

PowerPoint 2019 Quick Reference

from the book *Microsoft PowerPoint 2019 In 90 Pages* © Belleyre Books 2019

Quick Setup
- From the Start screen, click Blank Presentation or another template.
- Design tab to replace or edit the theme. *p. 12, 31*
- Design ⇨ Slide Size to change slide setup. *p. 12*

Presentation Views
- View ⇨ Normal for thumbnails and slides. *p. 29*
- View ⇨ Outline View for slide icons and text that can be dragged to reorder information. *p. 29*
- View ⇨ Slide Sorter for thumbnails that include timings, if any. *p. 29, 80, 83*
- View ⇨ Reading View to review your presentation. *p. 29*
- View ⇨ Notes Page for slides and speaker notes. *p. 27*
- View ⇨ Slide Master for making global changes to a theme. *p. 33*

Working with Slides
- Home ⇨ New Slide arrow and then select a layout to add a slide. *p. 13*
- Click a thumbnail and press the Delete key to remove a slide. *p. 14*
- Click in a slide placeholder to add content. *p. 15*
- Insert ⇨ Symbol to insert a character or symbol not on the keyboard. *p. 16, 17*
- On the Home tab, click Cut (Ctrl+X) or Copy (Ctrl+C) to remove or copy selected text or objects. *p. 19, 67-69*
- Home ⇨ Paste (Ctrl+V) to insert previously cut or copied text or objects. Click Paste Options to control formats. *p. 19, 67-69*
- Word text and tables and Excel cells and charts can also be copied and pasted (use Paste or Paste Special) for slide content. *pp. 67-69*
- Drag thumbnails up or down in Normal view to reorder slides. *p. 29*
- Home ⇨ Find for find and replace options. *p. 20*

Format Text & Placeholders
1. Select text or a placeholder.
2. Click commands on the mini toolbar. *p. 22*

Or

Click commands in the Font and Paragraph groups on the Home tab. *p. 22*

3. Change bullet level by clicking a Home tab level button. *p. 15*
4. Click the Shape Format tab to apply WordArt and other options. *p. 22-26*

To Copy Formats Select the text or placeholder with the formats you want to copy and click Home ⇨ Format Painter. Next, click the text or placeholder to receive the formats. *p. 26*

Presentation Design
- Use the Design tab to select a theme, variant, background, and slide size. *p. 31*
- Use the Transitions tab to create an effect when one slide changes to the next. *p. 36-39*
- Click in a bullet point or select an object and then use the Animations tab to apply an action. *p. 39-41*
- Insert ⇨ Table to add a table for displaying data. *p. 42*

Headers & Footers
1. Click Insert ⇨ Header & Footer. *p. 28*
2. Click the details to add and type text for the footer, if wanted. *p. 28*
3. Click Apply to update the current slide only; Click Apply to All to add the information to all slides.

Pictures
1. Click Insert ⇨ Pictures/Online Pictures. *p. 47*
2. Navigate to the image file or search for one online. *p. 47*
3. Use the Picture Format tab to format the image. *p. 49*

Microsoft and Microsoft PowerPoint are registered trademarks of the Microsoft Corporation.

Text Boxes
1. Click Insert ⇨ Text Box and then drag on the slide. *p. 52*
2. Click once inside the text box to type your text.
3. Use the Home tab and Shape Format tab to format text and shape style. *p. 53*

Shapes and Action Buttons
1. Click Insert ⇨ Shapes and then click a shape (Action Buttons are at the bottom of the gallery). *p. 54*
2. Drag on the slide to create the shape.
3. If a shape supports text, double-click the center, if needed, to display the insertion point and type the text. *p. 54*
4. If you added an Action Button, a dialog box is displayed for selecting the associated action. *p. 59*
5. Use the Home tab and Shape Format tab to format text and shape style. *p. 53*

SmartArt
1. Click Insert ⇨ SmartArt and select a graphic from the dialog box. *p. 56*
2. Click a text box to add text; click a photo icon to add an image. *p. 56*
3. Right-click a shape for options to Add Shape or Change Shape. *p. 57*
4. Use the SmartArt Design tab to format text and shape styles. *p. 57*
- Convert a bulleted list to SmartArt with right-click and then Convert to SmartArt.

Arrange and Edit Objects
- Click Home ⇨ Arrange ⇨ Selection Pane or Format ⇨ Selection Pane for a list of objects on a slide. *p. 20, 51*
- Use Format tab options to arrange selected objects. *p. 51*
- Use View tab options to display gridlines, guides, and a ruler to assist in manually placing objects. *p. 51*
- Point to an object and drag when the four-headed move pointer appears to move it. Drag a handle to size the object. Drag the circular rotation handle to rotate it. *p. 49*

Media Files
1. Click Insert ⇨ Video/Audio. *p. 59-66*
2. Use the Video/Audio Format tab and Video/Audio Playback tab to format the object frame and playback options. *p. 60-66*
3. For more audio options, click Animations ⇨ Animation Pane, click the arrow next to the audio object, and select Effect Options. *p. 41*

Speaker Notes
- Click Notes in the status bar to display a Notes pane on a slide. *p. 27*

Delivering a Presentation
1. Click Slide Show ⇨ From Beginning or Slide Show ⇨ Custom Slide Show or press Alt+F5 to go directly to Presenter View. *p. 77-78*
2. Use keyboard shortcuts (below) or controls to navigate through animations and slides. Controls display when you move the mouse to the lower-left of the slide. In Presenter View, controls are below the slide.
- If you want a slide show to run from timings, click Slide Show ⇨ Rehearse Timings to create timings (*p. 80*) and then select Slide Show ⇨ Use Timings before starting the show.

Recording a Presentation
1. Click Slide Show ⇨ Record Slide Show ⇨ Record From Beginning. *p. 82*
2. Use keyboard shortcuts (below) or controls below the slide to navigate through animations and slides.
3. If you want to distribute the video, click File ⇨ Export and then click Create a Video. *p. 83*

Keyboard Shortcuts *p. 30*
- **Next slide or animation**: spacebar, N, Enter, down arrow, right arrow, PgDn.
- **Previous slide or animation**: backspace, P, up arrow, left arrow, PgUp.
- **Display all slides**: Ctrl+S.
- **End slide show**: Esc

Microsoft and Microsoft PowerPoint are registered trademarks of the Microsoft Corporation.

Made in the USA
Coppell, TX
25 January 2022